Speaking CPE

Ten practice tests for the **Cambridge C2 Proficiency**

Luis Porras Wadley

PROSPERITY EDUCATION

www.prosperityeducation.net

Registered offices: Sherlock Close, Cambridge
CB3 0HP, United Kingdom

© Prosperity Education Ltd. 2022

First published 2022

ISBN: 978-1-913825-64-5

This publication is in copyright. Subject to statutory exception and to the provisions of relevant collective licensing agreements, no reproduction of any part may take place without the written permission of Prosperity Education.

'Cambridge C2 Proficiency' and 'CPE' are brands belonging to The Chancellor, Masters and Scholars of the University of Cambridge and are not associated with Prosperity Education or its products.

The moral rights of the author have been asserted.

Cover design and typesetting by ORP Cambridge

For further information and resources, visit:
www.prosperityeducation.net

To infinity and beyond.

Contents

Introduction 4

Cambridge C2 Proficiency: Speaking parts 5

Frequently asked questions 6

Test 1 9

Test 2 17

Test 3 25

Test 4 33

Test 5 41

Test 6 49

Test 7 57

Test 8 65

Test 9 73

Test 10 81

Model answers 89

Examiner's comments 97

Part 2 booklet (colour) download code 104

Introduction

The Cambridge C2 Proficiency examination, formerly known as the Certificate of Proficiency in English (CPE), is an examination developed by Cambridge Assessment English, which is part of the University of Cambridge.

The C2 Proficiency is usually taken by candidates who want to obtain a C2-level certificate, which corresponds to a globally native-like level of English. As described by the Common European Framework of Reference for Languages (CEFRL), candidates with a C2 level are considered *proficient users*, that is, users who show *mastery* or *comprehensive operational proficiency* of the English language, thus being able to:

- understand with ease virtually everything heard or read
- summarise information from different spoken and written sources, reconstructing arguments and accounts in a coherent presentation
- express themselves spontaneously, and very fluently and precisely, differentiating finer shades of meaning even in more complex situations.

The Speaking paper is one of the five papers that comprise the C2 Proficiency examination. This section of the exam is taken in pairs, or trios, of candidates, who are assessed by two examiners: the interlocutor and the assessor. The interlocutor is responsible for delivering the instructions, handling the test booklet and interacting with the candidates, while the assessor simply listens and marks each candidate's performance.

The Speaking paper is divided into three parts, each of which comprise a different task. Different degrees of participation are expected from the candidates in each of these tasks.

This book aims to provide meaningful speaking practice while following the format of the C1 Advanced Speaking paper. Both teachers and candidates can benefit from this resource, in that they can familiarise themselves with the format and level of the exam, and the type of questions and topics covered. Furthermore, and most importantly, students can learn, through repetitive practice, what to expect on the day of their Speaking test.

I hope that you will find this resource a useful study aid, and I wish you all the best in preparing for the C2 Proficiency examination.

Luis Porras Wadley

Granada, 2022

Luis Porras Wadley is the owner and director of KSE Academy, an English academy and official Cambridge Exam Preparation Centre based in Granada. As an English teacher, Luis has been preparing Cambridge candidates successfully more than ten years.

© Prosperity Education 2022 | 'Cambridge C2 Proficiency' and 'CPE' are brands belonging to The Chancellor, Masters and Scholars of the University of Cambridge and are not associated with Prosperity Education or its products.

C2 Proficiency: Speaking parts

In **Part 1**, candidates are asked questions mainly about themselves, their background and their experiences. It starts with a set of brief introductory questions (e.g. *...and your names are? Where are you from?*) and continues with one or more topic-based questions. These topics may include things like holidays and travel, leisure-time activities, friends and family, television, etc. In responding to these questions, candidates are expected to provide brief but complete answers.

Timing	2 minutes (pair) / 3 minutes (trio)
Focus	Giving personal information, expressing opinions about various topics, and talking about past experiences and plans for the future.
Interaction	Interlocutor – Candidate

Part 2, which is divided into two tasks, is the main collaborative part of the test. In this part, candidates are expected to have a two-way conversation during which they should exchange views, opinions and information through collaboration and negotiation. For the first task, candidates are given several photographs and are asked to react to two of them based on some brief instructions (e.g. *...look at pictures * and * and talk together about how common these situations are when going on a trip*). Candidates have one minute to speak together. In the second task, which lasts three minutes, candidates are presented with a hypothetical situation in which the images or their topics represent something important. Candidates are then asked to develop a three-minute discussion about what all the pictures represent, and to make a decision or put forward a suggestion based on their discussion.

Timing	Total: 4 minutes (pair) / 6 minutes (trio) Task 1 – Introductory discussion: 1 minute (pair) / 2 minutes (trio) Task 2 – Long discussion: 3 minutes (pair) / 4 minutes (trio)
Focus	Discussing, exchanging ideas, agreeing and disagreeing, asking for opinions, explaining views, justifying opinions, reaching agreements, making decisions, suggesting ideas, speculating, negotiating, etc.
Interaction	Interlocutor – Candidate – Candidate

Part 3, which also comprises two different tasks, is the main 'individual' part of the exam, although there some candidate interaction is still expected. Also, it is important to know that this entire part revolves around one core topic (e.g. *Trust*). In the first task, one of the candidates is given a card with a question and three prompts. He/she is then asked to talk about the topic on the card for about two minutes. When the two minutes are over, a short discussion will begin. The examiner will ask the second candidate a follow-up question, and then invite the first candidate to join in too (e.g. *What do you think?*). After approximately one minute, it is the other candidate's turn to be given a card, and the task will begin again. After both turns are over, the examiner will move on to the last task of the test, which consists of a set of questions that stem from the main discussion topic (e.g. *Trust*). The candidates are expected to develop extended answers, and may be prompted to exchange views rather than answer individually.

Timing	Total: 10 minutes (pair) / 15 minutes (trio) Task 1 – Long turn: 2 minutes (per candidate's turn) Task 2 – Short discussion: 1 minute (per candidate's turn) Task 3 – Final discussion: 4 minutes
Focus	Imparting information, organising longer speech, expressing and justifying opinions, agreeing and disagreeing, evaluating, etc.
Interaction	Interlocutor – Candidate – Candidate

© Prosperity Education 2022 | 'Cambridge C2 Proficiency' and 'CPE' are brands belonging to The Chancellor, Masters and Scholars of the University of Cambridge and are not associated with Prosperity Education or its products.

Cambridge C2 Proficiency: Speaking

Is the Speaking test taken individually or in pairs? The Speaking test is taken in pairs or trios, unless a candidate has special needs that may affect their performance. This may lead to them taking the test individually. However, regular tests are normally taken in pairs, and if there is an uneven number of candidates, only the last three candidates will take the test as a trio.

How long is the Speaking test? Normally, the Speaking exam will last around 16 minutes. However, when taken as a trio, the test will last around 24 minutes, so that all candidates have the same chance to speak as if they were in a regular pair-format test.

Can candidates choose to do the test with a friend or classmate? This depends on the examination centre candidates register with. Each centre has its own policies and so this may or may not be allowed. In the end, it is up to the supervisor of the exam session to allow it or not, and the decision will be based on exam timing and logistics rather than candidates' preferences.

Do candidates have to speak with each other at some point? Yes, they do. Candidates must always speak to each other in Part 2 and will usually do so in Part 3. The only part that is entirely carried out individually is Part 1. However, in their answers, candidates can refer to what the other candidate has said earlier in the test if they feel it is relevant.

How many people are there in the examination room? In the examination room there can be up to five people: two examiners and two or three candidates. Occasionally, there may be a third examiner, but their role will not be to assess the candidates.

What happens if the interlocutor interrupts a candidate when the time allocated to a task is up? This is completely normal, and candidates should expect to be interrupted when the time is up. The interlocutor's job involves ensuring that every candidate has the same opportunities to speak, which includes having the same time allocated to do so. If a candidate has developed their answer well and has responded fully, but with time to spare, they will not lose marks.

In Part 2, do candidates need to talk about all the pictures? No, this is not necessary, although it should not be a problem to do so given the timing for each task. The prompts in this part of the test are given to ensure that candidates have some ideas to talk about, and that they engage in a real discussion. However, they are not assessed on whether they talk about all of them; it is the quality of the language used when working towards a decision or solution that matters.

In Part 2, will the instructions or questions be written above the visual prompts? No, they will not. Unlike in other Speaking tests, such as the C1 Advanced or B2 First that have parts based on visual prompts, Part 2 of the C2 Proficiency Speaking test simply presents the main topic of the discussion (E.g.: *Insurance companies – Travel*), so it is extremely important to listen to the interlocutor's instructions carefully and, if necessary, ask him or her to repeat them.

In Part 2, must candidates reach an agreement by the end of the task? Not at all. The purpose of the test is to assess candidates' speaking skills, not the completion of the task or the conveyance of their opinions. Candidates are only expected to develop a discussion in which they work towards an agreement or decision by means of exchanging views and opinions, and agreeing and disagreeing. Whether or not they have reached an agreement by the end of the task is irrelevant to the awarding of their mark.

In Part 3, do candidates have time to think before their two-minute-long turn? Even though the interlocutor will not say so, each candidate has up to ten seconds to look at their card before they begin. If necessary, after those ten seconds, the interlocutor will prompt the candidate to start speaking by saying *Would you like to begin now?*.

© Prosperity Education 2022 | 'Cambridge C2 Proficiency' and 'CPE' are brands belonging to The Chancellor, Masters and Scholars of the University of Cambridge and are not associated with Prosperity Education or its products.

Frequently asked questions

In Part 3, do candidates have to talk about all the different prompts? No, this is not necessary. The prompts in this part of the test are there to ensure that candidates have some ideas to talk about, and that they engage in a discussion. However, they are not necessarily expected to use all of them, nor are they limited to those prompts; they can bring their own ideas into the discussion.

What do candidates need to take with them to the Speaking test? Candidates need to take a valid form of photographic ID (Passport, Identity Card, Driver's Licence, etc.) and their Confirmation of Entry, which is a document provided by the examination centre some time before the test.

What are the mark sheets mentioned at the beginning of the exams? The mark sheets contain each candidate's name, surname and their candidate number, and this is where the assessor writes their marks. These sheets are given to candidates before they enter the examination room, and they will have to give them to the interlocutor at the beginning of the test. The examiners will then keep the mark sheets to relay the candidates' marks to Cambridge Assessment English.

Where does the Speaking exam take place? The Speaking exam can take place in a range of venues, but it is most likely to take place in the examination centre itself (usually a language school) or one of its examination venues, which also tend to be language schools and, sometimes, hotels or conference rooms.

Is the Speaking exam done the same day as the other parts of the test? Not normally, but it can happen. Given the length of the whole exam, it is usually more practical and reasonable to do the Speaking test on a different day. This is decided by the examination centres and candidates are informed of this well in advance.

Will the examiners be looking at the candidates throughout the whole test? No, they will not. Examiners, especially the assessors, have to assign marks while the exam is taking place. For this reason, there will be times throughout the test when they might be looking at their examiner booklets or candidate mark sheets instead of the candidates. However, this does not mean that they are not paying attention to the candidates and their responses!

How is the Speaking exam marked? Each candidate's performance is marked both by the interlocutor and the assessor, who give candidates a score for six different categories: grammatical resource, lexical resource, discourse management, pronunciation, interactive communication and global achievement. The assessor is responsible for assessing the first five categories, which account for two thirds of the score, and the interlocutor awards the global mark, which comprises one third of the final speaking score.

Can another candidate's performance affect a candidate's score? No, it cannot. Although the exam is taken in pairs or trios, candidates are assessed individually and examiners are duly trained to do so, ensuring that both candidates have the same opportunities to speak and thus can be marked separately.

Can candidates memorise some answers for the exam? While the introductory questions in Part 1 are common to all tests, candidates are advised not to prepare long answers in advance or to memorise short speeches. Examiners can easily tell when a candidate is using a pre-learned speech, and will interrupt them when they feel it is necessary to do so.

Is the candidates' pronunciation expected to be native-like? No, it is not. First-language interference is expected and not penalised if it does not hinder communication. However, at this level, candidates are expected to be fully intelligible and have great control of phonological features like intonation, stress and articulation, and be able to use these features to convey and enhance meaning effectively.

© Prosperity Education 2022 | 'Cambridge C2 Proficiency' and 'CPE' are brands belonging to The Chancellor, Masters and Scholars of the University of Cambridge and are not associated with Prosperity Education or its products.

Cambridge C2 Proficiency Speaking

Test 1

© Prosperity Education 2022 | 'Cambridge C2 Proficiency' and 'CPE' are brands belonging to The Chancellor, Masters and Scholars of the University of Cambridge and are not associated with Prosperity Education or its products.

Candidates' background

Interlocutor

Good morning/afternoon/evening. My name is .... and this is my colleague ....

And your names are?

Could I have your mark sheets, please?

Thank you.

First of all, we'd like to know something about you.

- **Where are you from** *(Candidate A)***? And you** *(Candidate B)***?**
- *[Address Candidate B]* **Are you working or studying at the moment?**
- *[Address Candidate A]* **And you?**

Select a further question for each candidate:

- **You said you're from** *(candidate's home town/area)*. **How do you like it there?**
- **What kind of job would you like to have in the future? ...... (Why?)**
- **Would you rather spend your free time with your friends or your family? ...... (Why?)**
- **Can you tell us something about the area where you live?**
- **What would be your ideal holiday destination? ...... (Why?)**
- **How much time do you spend watching television? ...... (Why?)**

Candidates

....

Interlocutor

Thank you.

© Prosperity Education 2022 | 'Cambridge C2 Proficiency' and 'CPE' are brands belonging to The Chancellor, Masters and Scholars of the University of Cambridge and are not associated with Prosperity Education or its products.

1 Insurance company – Travel

Interlocutor **Now, in this part of the test you're going to do something together. Here are some pictures of people in different situations.**

*Place **Part 2** booklet in front of the candidates. Select **two** of the pictures for the candidates to look at.*

First, I'd like you to look at pictures * and * and talk together about how common these situations are when going on a trip.

You have about a minute for this, so don't worry if I interrupt you.

Candidates

....

1 minute (2 minutes for groups of three)

Interlocutor **Thank you. Now look at all the pictures.**

I'd like you to imagine that a group of entrepreneurs is setting up a new travel-insurance company. These pictures show common concerns or problems that people have when travelling.

Talk together about how an insurance company can help to provide solutions to these situations. Then suggest which of these problems should be the main focus of the new insurance company.

You have about three minutes to talk about this.

Candidates

....

Approximately 3 minutes (4 minutes for groups of three)

Interlocutor **Thank you. (Can I have the booklet, please?)** *Retrieve **Part** 2 booklet.*

© Prosperity Education 2022 | 'Cambridge C2 Proficiency' and 'CPE' are brands belonging to The Chancellor, Masters and Scholars of the University of Cambridge and are not associated with Prosperity Education or its products.

1 Insurance company – Travel

© Prosperity Education 2022 | 'Cambridge C2 Proficiency' and 'CPE' are brands belonging to The Chancellor, Masters and Scholars of the University of Cambridge and are not associated with Prosperity Education or its products.

Trust

Interlocutor

Now, in this part of the test you're each going to talk on your own for about two minutes.

You need to listen while your partner is speaking because you'll be asked to comment afterwards.

So *(Candidate A)*, **I'm going to give you a card with a question written on it, and I'd like you to tell us what you think. There are also some ideas on the card for you to use if you like.**

All right? Here is your card.

*Place **Part 3** booklet, **Task 1(a)**, in front of Candidate A.*

Please let *(Candidate B)* **see your card. Remember** *(Candidate A)*, **you have about two minutes to talk before we join in.**

Allow up to 10 seconds before saying, if necessary: **Would you like to begin now?**

Candidate A

....

2 minutes

Interlocutor **Thank you.**

Interlocutor *Ask **one** of the following questions to Candidate B:*

- **Do you find it easy to trust other people? ..... (Why? / Why not?)**
- **What do you think can be done to regain someone's trust?**
- **Can you really be friends with someone you can't trust entirely? ..... (Why? / Why not?)**

Invite Candidate A to join in by selecting one of the following prompts:

- **What do you think?**
- **Do you agree?**
- **How about you?**

Candidates

....

1 minute

Interlocutor **Thank you. (Can I have the booklet, please?)** *Retrieve **Part 3** booklet.*

© Prosperity Education 2022 | 'Cambridge C2 Proficiency' and 'CPE' are brands belonging to The Chancellor, Masters and Scholars of the University of Cambridge and are not associated with Prosperity Education or its products.

Trust – continued

Interlocutor **Now** *(Candidate B),* **it's your turn to be given a question. Here is your card.**

*Place **Part 3** booklet, **Task 1(b)**, in front of Candidate B.*

Please let *(Candidate A)* **see your card. Remember** *(Candidate B)*, **you have about two minutes to tell us what you think, and there are some ideas on the card for you to use if you like. All right?**

Allow up to 10 seconds before saying, if necessary: **Would you like to begin now?**

Candidate B

....

2 minutes

Interlocutor **Thank you.**

Interlocutor *Ask **one** of the following questions to Candidate A:*

- **In general, do you think politicians are trustworthy? ..... (Why? / Why not?)**
- **Why do you think some people don't trust the media nowadays?**
- **Should we always trust scientific research? ..... (Why? / Why not?)**

Invite Candidate B to join in by selecting one of the following prompts:
- **What do you think?**
- **Do you agree?**
- **How about you?**

Candidates

....

1 minute

Interlocutor **Thank you. (Can I have the booklet, please?)** *Retrieve **Part 3** booklet.*

Interlocutor **Now, to finish the test, we're going to talk about 'trust' in general.**

Address a selection of the following questions to both candidates:

- **Can you always trust what you read online? ..... (Why? / Why not?)**
- **What part does the internet play in the emergence of conspiracy theories?**
- **How does misinformation contribute to the public's distrust of news sources?**
- **What can we do to make sure that we choose reliable news sources?**
- **Why do you think misinformation seems to spread faster than real facts?**
- **To what extent do family and friends influence what information we trust?**

Interlocutor Thank you. That is the end of the test.

© Prosperity Education 2022 | 'Cambridge C2 Proficiency' and 'CPE' are brands belonging to The Chancellor, Masters and Scholars of the University of Cambridge and are not associated with Prosperity Education or its products.

Task 1(a)

Why is it important to be able to trust the people in our life?

- **colleagues**
- **friends**
- **family**

Task 1(b)

What can happen when you lose trust in someone or something?

- **the media**
- **politicians**
- **science**

© Prosperity Education 2022 | 'Cambridge C2 Proficiency' and 'CPE' are brands belonging to The Chancellor, Masters and Scholars of the University of Cambridge and are not associated with Prosperity Education or its products.

Date	DD	MM	YY

Candidate ______________________________

Marks available

Grammatical Resource	0	1	1.5	2	2.5	3	3.5	4	4.5	5
Lexical Resource	0	1	1.5	2	2.5	3	3.5	4	4.5	5
Discourse Management	0	1	1.5	2	2.5	3	3.5	4	4.5	5
Pronunciation	0	1	1.5	2	2.5	3	3.5	4	4.5	5
Interactive Communication	0	1	1.5	2	2.5	3	3.5	4	4.5	5
Global Achievement	0	1	1.5	2	2.5	3	3.5	4	4.5	5

Item descriptors

Grammatical Resource *Control* *Range*	• Degree of control of grammatical forms. • Range of grammatical forms used.
Lexical Resource *Range* *Appropriacy*	• Range of vocabulary used to give and exchange views. • Appropriacy of vocabulary used.
Discourse Management *Extent* *Relevance* *Coherence* *Cohesion*	• Stretches of language produced. • Relevance of contributions and organisation of ideas. • Use of appropriate cohesive devices and discourse markers.
Pronunciation *Intonation* *Stress* *Individual sounds*	• Intelligibility • Intonation • Word stress • Individual sounds
Interactive Communication *Initiating* *Responding* *Development*	• Initiating, responding and linking contributions to other speakers' interventions. • Maintaining and developing interaction, and negotiating towards an outcome. • Widening the scope of the interaction.

© Prosperity Education 2022 | 'Cambridge C2 Proficiency' and 'CPE' are brands belonging to The Chancellor, Masters and Scholars of the University of Cambridge and are not associated with Prosperity Education or its products.

Cambridge C2 Proficiency Speaking

Test 2

© Prosperity Education 2022 | 'Cambridge C2 Proficiency' and 'CPE' are brands belonging to The Chancellor, Masters and Scholars of the University of Cambridge and are not associated with Prosperity Education or its products.

Candidates' background

Interlocutor Good morning/afternoon/evening. My name is .... and this is my colleague ....

And your names are?

Could I have your mark sheets, please?

Thank you.

First of all, we'd like to know something about you.

- **Where are you from** *(Candidate A)***? And you** *(Candidate B)***?**
- *[Address Candidate B]* **Are you working or studying at the moment?**
- *[Address Candidate A]* **And you?**

Select a further question for each candidate:

- **What country would you visit if you had the chance? ...... (Why?)**
- **Would you like to have more free time than you have nowadays? ...... (Why? / Why not?)**
- **Would you like to live abroad permanently? ...... (Why? / Why not?)**
- **What do you enjoy about learning foreign languages?**
- **How do you think English will benefit you in the future?**
- **What kind of job would you like to have in the future? ...... (Why? / Why not?)**

Candidates

....

Interlocutor **Thank you.**

© Prosperity Education 2022 | 'Cambridge C2 Proficiency' and 'CPE' are brands belonging to The Chancellor, Masters and Scholars of the University of Cambridge and are not associated with Prosperity Education or its products.

1 Magazine article – New technologies

Interlocutor **Now, in this part of the test you're going to do something together. Here are some pictures of people in different situations.**

*Place **Part 2** booklet in front of the candidates. Select **two** of the pictures for the candidates to look at.*

First, I'd like you to look at pictures * and * and talk together about what the people might be using their devices for.

You have about a minute for this, so don't worry if I interrupt you.

Candidates

....

1 minute (2 minutes for groups of three)

Interlocutor **Thank you. Now look at all the pictures.**

I'd like you to imagine that a magazine is going to publish an article on new technologies and how people use them nowadays. Some of these pictures will be used alongside the article text.

Talk together about the value of new technologies as shown in these pictures. Then suggest which picture should <u>not</u> be included in the article.

You have about three minutes to talk about this.

Candidates

....

Approximately 3 minutes (4 minutes for groups of three)

Interlocutor **Thank you. (Can I have the booklet, please?)** *Retrieve **Part 2** booklet.*

© Prosperity Education 2022 | 'Cambridge C2 Proficiency' and 'CPE' are brands belonging to The Chancellor, Masters and Scholars of the University of Cambridge and are not associated with Prosperity Education or its products.

1 Magazine article – New technologies

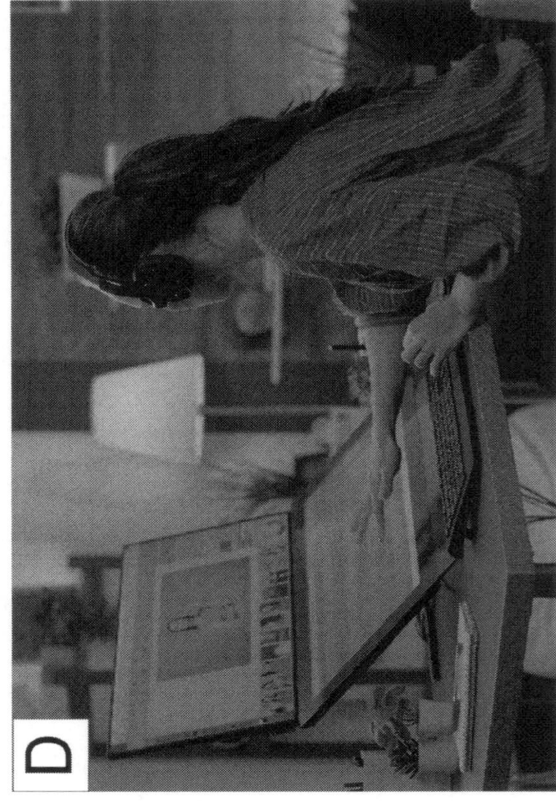

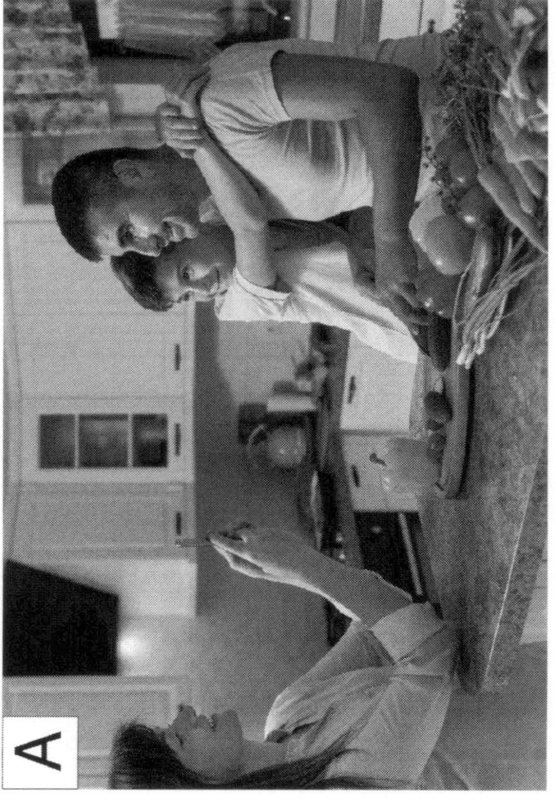

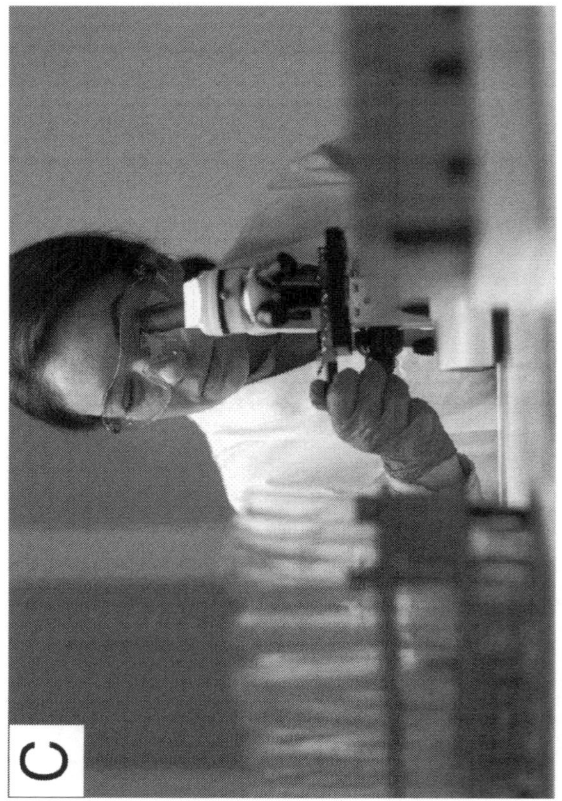

© Prosperity Education 2022 | 'Cambridge C2 Proficiency' and 'CPE' are brands belonging to The Chancellor, Masters and Scholars of the University of Cambridge and are not associated with Prosperity Education or its products.

Time

Interlocutor

Now, in this part of the test you're each going to talk on your own for about two minutes.

You need to listen while your partner is speaking because you'll be asked to comment afterwards.

So *(Candidate A)*, **I'm going to give you a card with a question written on it, and I'd like you to tell us what you think. There are also some ideas on the card for you to use if you like.**

All right? Here is your card.

*Place **Part 3** booklet, **Task 1(a)**, in front of Candidate A.*

Please let *(Candidate B)* **see your card. Remember** *(Candidate A)*, **you have about two minutes to talk before we join in.**

Allow up to 10 seconds before saying, if necessary: **Would you like to begin now?**

Candidate A

....

2 minutes

Interlocutor **Thank you.**

Interlocutor *Ask **one** of the following questions to Candidate B:*

- **Do you feel that you manage your time efficiently? ...... (Why? / Why not?)**
- **What can people do to improve their time-management skills?**
- **Does work efficiency depend entirely on time-management? ...... (Why? / Why not?)**

Invite Candidate A to join in by selecting one of the following prompts:

- **What do you think?**
- **Do you agree?**
- **How about you?**

Candidates

....

1 minute

Interlocutor **Thank you. (Can I have the booklet, please?)** *Retrieve **Part 3** booklet.*

© Prosperity Education 2022 | 'Cambridge C2 Proficiency' and 'CPE' are brands belonging to The Chancellor, Masters and Scholars of the University of Cambridge and are not associated with Prosperity Education or its products.

Time – continued

Interlocutor **Now** *(Candidate B),* **it's your turn to be given a question. Here is your card.**

*Place **Part 3** booklet, **Task 1(b)**, in front of Candidate B.*

Please let *(Candidate A)* **see your card. Remember** *(Candidate B)*, **you have about two minutes to tell us what you think, and there are some ideas on the card for you to use if you like. All right?**

Allow up to 10 seconds before saying, if necessary: **Would you like to begin now?**

Candidate B

....

2 minutes

Interlocutor **Thank you.**

Interlocutor *Ask **one** of the following questions to Candidate A:*

- **Why is it important to make the most of the time we have?**
- **Is nostalgia a direct result of time passing by? ...... (Why? / Why not?)**
- **Is it true that we don't realise the passage of time until it's too late?**

Invite Candidate B to join in by selecting one of the following prompts:
- **What do you think?**
- **Do you agree?**
- **How about you?**

Candidates

....

1 minute

Interlocutor **Thank you. (Can I have the booklet, please?)** *Retrieve **Part 3** booklet.*

Interlocutor **Now, to finish the test, we're going to talk about 'time' in general.**

Address a selection of the following questions to both candidates:

- **Why do people say that time passes by more quickly as we get older?**
- **Do some people focus too much on the past? ..... (Why? / Why not?)**
- **To what extent does society encourage people to focus on the present?**
- **Is the world a better place now than in the past? ..... (Why? / Why not?)**
- **In your view, how important is it to plan for the future? ..... (Why? / Why not?)**
- **Some people say that time is money. What do you think?**

Interlocutor Thank you. That is the end of the test.

© Prosperity Education 2022 | 'Cambridge C2 Proficiency' and 'CPE' are brands belonging to The Chancellor, Masters and Scholars of the University of Cambridge and are not associated with Prosperity Education or its products.

Task 1(a)

How can efficient time-management help us in our daily lives?

- **work**
- **leisure**
- **studies**

Task 1(b)

How do different people regard the passage of time?

- **childhood**
- **adulthood**
- **old age**

© Prosperity Education 2022 | 'Cambridge C2 Proficiency' and 'CPE' are brands belonging to The Chancellor, Masters and Scholars of the University of Cambridge and are not associated with Prosperity Education or its products.

Date	DD	MM	YY

Candidate ____________________

Marks available

Grammatical Resource	0	1	1.5	2	2.5	3	3.5	4	4.5	5
Lexical Resource	0	1	1.5	2	2.5	3	3.5	4	4.5	5
Discourse Management	0	1	1.5	2	2.5	3	3.5	4	4.5	5
Pronunciation	0	1	1.5	2	2.5	3	3.5	4	4.5	5
Interactive Communication	0	1	1.5	2	2.5	3	3.5	4	4.5	5
Global Achievement	0	1	1.5	2	2.5	3	3.5	4	4.5	5

Item descriptors

Grammatical Resource *Control* *Range*	• Degree of control of grammatical forms. • Range of grammatical forms used.
Lexical Resource *Range* *Appropriacy*	• Range of vocabulary used to give and exchange views. • Appropriacy of vocabulary used.
Discourse Management *Extent* *Relevance* *Coherence* *Cohesion*	• Stretches of language produced. • Relevance of contributions and organisation of ideas. • Use of appropriate cohesive devices and discourse markers.
Pronunciation *Intonation* *Stress* *Individual sounds*	• Intelligibility • Intonation • Word stress • Individual sounds
Interactive Communication *Initiating* *Responding* *Development*	• Initiating, responding and linking contributions to other speakers' interventions. • Maintaining and developing interaction, and negotiating towards an outcome. • Widening the scope of the interaction.

© Prosperity Education 2022 | 'Cambridge C2 Proficiency' and 'CPE' are brands belonging to The Chancellor, Masters and Scholars of the University of Cambridge and are not associated with Prosperity Education or its products.

Cambridge C2 Proficiency Speaking

Test 3

© Prosperity Education 2022 | 'Cambridge C2 Proficiency' and 'CPE' are brands belonging to The Chancellor, Masters and Scholars of the University of Cambridge and are not associated with Prosperity Education or its products.

Candidates' background

Interlocutor

Good morning/afternoon/evening. My name is .... and this is my colleague ....

And your names are?

Could I have your mark sheets, please?

Thank you.

First of all, we'd like to know something about you.

- **Where are you from** *(Candidate A)***? And you** *(Candidate B)***?**
- *[Address Candidate B]* **Are you working or studying at the moment?**
- *[Address Candidate A]* **And you?**

Select a further question for each candidate:

- **If you had to move abroad, what would you miss about your home country?**
- **Are you interested in new technologies? ...... (Why? / Why not?)**
- **How much time do you spend on social media?**
- **What kind of books do you like to read?**
- **How would you describe your own country to a visitor?**
- **Would you rather read a book on paper or on an electronic device? ...... (Why?)**

Candidates

....

Interlocutor

Thank you.

© Prosperity Education 2022 | 'Cambridge C2 Proficiency' and 'CPE' are brands belonging to The Chancellor, Masters and Scholars of the University of Cambridge and are not associated with Prosperity Education or its products.

1 Book – Learning styles

Interlocutor

Now, in this part of the test, you're going to do something together. Here are some pictures of people in different situations.

*Place **Part 2** booklet in front of the candidates. Select **two** of the pictures for the candidates to look at.*

First, I'd like you to look at pictures * and * and talk together about what the people might be learning in each situation.

You have about a minute for this, so don't worry if I interrupt you.

Candidates

....

1 minute (2 minutes for groups of three)

Interlocutor

Thank you. Now look at all the pictures.

I'd like you to imagine that an author is writing a book about different learning styles. These pictures will be used to illustrate the book.

Talk together about how people can benefit from the ways of learning depicted in these pictures. Then suggest two other ways of learning things that should appear in the book.

You have about three minutes to talk about this.

Candidates

....

Approximately 3 minutes (4 minutes for groups of three)

Interlocutor

Thank you. (Can I have the booklet, please?) *Retrieve **Part** 2 booklet.*

© Prosperity Education 2022 | 'Cambridge C2 Proficiency' and 'CPE' are brands belonging to The Chancellor, Masters and Scholars of the University of Cambridge and are not associated with Prosperity Education or its products.

1 Book – Learning styles

B

D

A

C

© Prosperity Education 2022 | 'Cambridge C2 Proficiency' and 'CPE' are brands belonging to The Chancellor, Masters and Scholars of the University of Cambridge and are not associated with Prosperity Education or its products.

Changes

Interlocutor **Now, in this part of the test you're each going to talk on your own for about two minutes.**

You need to listen while your partner is speaking because you'll be asked to comment afterwards.

So *(Candidate A)*, **I'm going to give you a card with a question written on it, and I'd like you to tell us what you think. There are also some ideas on the card for you to use if you like.**

All right? Here is your card.

*Place **Part 3** booklet, **Task 1(a)**, in front of Candidate A.*

Please let *(Candidate B)* **see your card. Remember** *(Candidate A)*, **you have about two minutes to talk before we join in.**

Allow up to 10 seconds before saying, if necessary: **Would you like to begin now?**

Candidate A

....

2 minutes

Interlocutor **Thank you.**

Interlocutor *Ask **one** of the following questions to Candidate B:*

- **Is it possible to change someone's personality? ..... (Why? / Why not?)**
- **Should we always seek change in our lives? ..... (Why? / Why not?)**
- **Is it advisable to switch careers more than once? ..... (Why? / Why not?)**

Invite Candidate A to join in by selecting one of the following prompts:

- **What do you think?**
- **Do you agree?**
- **How about you?**

Candidates

....

1 minute

Interlocutor **Thank you. (Can I have the booklet, please?)** *Retrieve **Part 3** booklet.*

© Prosperity Education 2022 | 'Cambridge C2 Proficiency' and 'CPE' are brands belonging to The Chancellor, Masters and Scholars of the University of Cambridge and are not associated with Prosperity Education or its products.

Changes – continued

Interlocutor **Now** *(Candidate B)*, **it's your turn to be given a question. Here is your card.**

*Place **Part 3** booklet, **Task 1(b)**, in front of Candidate B.*

Please let *(Candidate A)* **see your card. Remember** *(Candidate B)*, **you have about two minutes to tell us what you think, and there are some ideas on the card for you to use if you like. All right?**

Allow up to 10 seconds before saying, if necessary: **Would you like to begin now?**

Candidate B

....

2 minutes

Interlocutor **Thank you.**

Interlocutor *Ask **one** of the following questions to Candidate A:*

- **What can be done to help others to accept major changes?**
- **What do you think about people who don't want anything to change?**
- **Can positive changes have negative consequences? ..... (Why? / Why not?)**

> *Invite Candidate B to join in by selecting one of the following prompts:*
> - **What do you think?**
> - **Do you agree?**
> - **How about you?**

Candidates

....

1 minute

Interlocutor **Thank you. (Can I have the booklet, please?)** *Retrieve **Part** 3 booklet.*

Interlocutor **Now, to finish the test, we're going to talk about 'changes' in general.**

Address a selection of the following questions to both candidates:

- **Why do you think some people seek change while others resist it?**
- **What are some changes that people may find difficult to adapt to?**
- **Some people refuse to let traditions die out. Why do you think that is?**
- **Is it okay to change your opinion on important matters? ..... (Why? / Why not?)**
- **Should someone change the way they dress to make a better impression?**
- **Is there anything you would change about society at present?**

Interlocutor Thank you. That is the end of the test.

© Prosperity Education 2022 | 'Cambridge C2 Proficiency' and 'CPE' are brands belonging to The Chancellor, Masters and Scholars of the University of Cambridge and are not associated with Prosperity Education or its products.

Task 1(a)

How do people change throughout their lives?

- **goals**
- **priorities**
- **friends**

Task 1(b)

How easy or difficult is it for people to accept the changes happening around them?

- **children**
- **adults**
- **the elderly**

© Prosperity Education 2022 | 'Cambridge C2 Proficiency' and 'CPE' are brands belonging to The Chancellor, Masters and Scholars of the University of Cambridge and are not associated with Prosperity Education or its products.

Date	DD	MM	YY

Candidate ______________________

Marks available

Grammatical Resource	0	1	1.5	2	2.5	3	3.5	4	4.5	5
Lexical Resource	0	1	1.5	2	2.5	3	3.5	4	4.5	5
Discourse Management	0	1	1.5	2	2.5	3	3.5	4	4.5	5
Pronunciation	0	1	1.5	2	2.5	3	3.5	4	4.5	5
Interactive Communication	0	1	1.5	2	2.5	3	3.5	4	4.5	5
Global Achievement	0	1	1.5	2	2.5	3	3.5	4	4.5	5

Item descriptors

Grammatical Resource *Control* *Range*	• Degree of control of grammatical forms. • Range of grammatical forms used.
Lexical Resource *Range* *Appropriacy*	• Range of vocabulary used to give and exchange views. • Appropriacy of vocabulary used.
Discourse Management *Extent* *Relevance* *Coherence* *Cohesion*	• Stretches of language produced. • Relevance of contributions and organisation of ideas. • Use of appropriate cohesive devices and discourse markers.
Pronunciation *Intonation* *Stress* *Individual sounds*	• Intelligibility • Intonation • Word stress • Individual sounds
Interactive Communication *Initiating* *Responding* *Development*	• Initiating, responding and linking contributions to other speakers' interventions. • Maintaining and developing interaction, and negotiating towards an outcome. • Widening the scope of the interaction.

© Prosperity Education 2022 | 'Cambridge C2 Proficiency' and 'CPE' are brands belonging to The Chancellor, Masters and Scholars of the University of Cambridge and are not associated with Prosperity Education or its products.

Cambridge C2 Proficiency Speaking

Test 4

© Prosperity Education 2022 | 'Cambridge C2 Proficiency' and 'CPE' are brands belonging to The Chancellor, Masters and Scholars of the University of Cambridge and are not associated with Prosperity Education or its products.

Candidates' background

Interlocutor

Good morning/afternoon/evening. My name is .... and this is my colleague ....

And your names are?

Could I have your mark sheets, please?

Thank you.

First of all, we'd like to know something about you.

- **Where are you from** *(Candidate A)***? And you** *(Candidate B)***?**
- *[Address Candidate B]* **Are you working or studying at the moment?**
- *[Address Candidate A]* **And you?**

Select a further question for each candidate:

- **How much interest do you take in current affairs? ...... (Why? / Why not?)**
- **Is music an important part of your life? ...... (Why? / Why not?)**
- **What would your ideal job be?**
- **What's something that you would really like to achieve in the near future?**
- **How important is the internet for your work or studies?**
- **What do you enjoy most about the English language?**

Candidates

....

Interlocutor

Thank you.

© Prosperity Education 2022 | 'Cambridge C2 Proficiency' and 'CPE' are brands belonging to The Chancellor, Masters and Scholars of the University of Cambridge and are not associated with Prosperity Education or its products.

1 Health article – Preventive therapies

Interlocutor

Now, in this part of the test, you're going to do something together. Here are some pictures of people in different situations.

Place ***Part 2*** *booklet in front of the candidates. Select* ***two*** *of the pictures for the candidates to look at.*

First, I'd like you to look at pictures * and * and talk together about how the people are looking after their health in each picture.

You have about a minute for this, so don't worry if I interrupt you.

Candidates

....

1 minute (2 minutes for groups of three)

Interlocutor

Thank you. Now look at all the pictures.

I'd like you to imagine that a health website is going to publish a new article about the importance of preventive therapies. These pictures will be used to illustrate the article.

Talk together about how effective the methods shown in the pictures can be to prevent some illnesses. Then decide which one should be the main picture of the article.

You have about three minutes to talk about this.

Candidates

....

Approximately 3 minutes (4 minutes for groups of three)

Interlocutor

Thank you. (Can I have the booklet, please?) *Retrieve* ***Part*** *2 booklet.*

© Prosperity Education 2022 | 'Cambridge C2 Proficiency' and 'CPE' are brands belonging to The Chancellor, Masters and Scholars of the University of Cambridge and are not associated with Prosperity Education or its products.

1 Health article – Preventive therapies

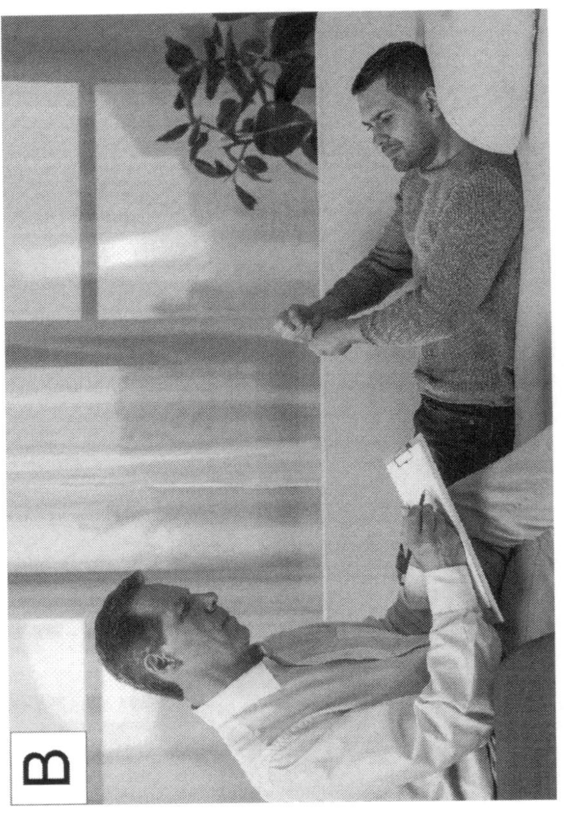
B

D

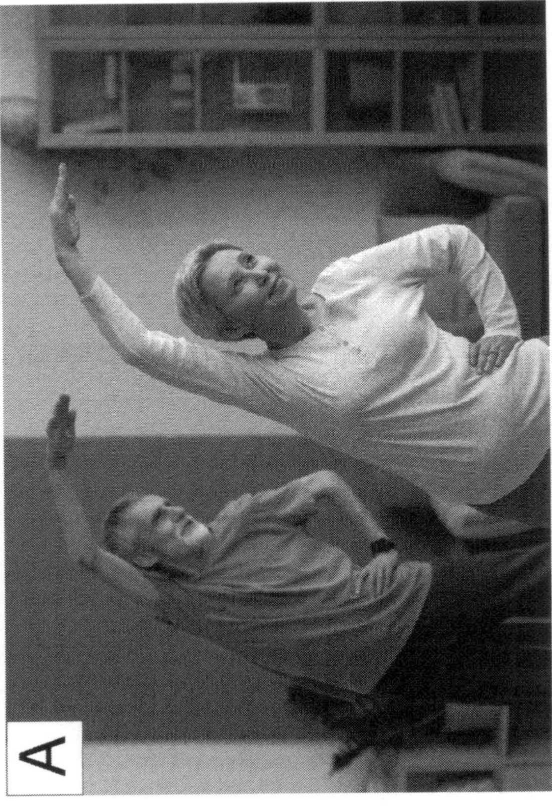
A

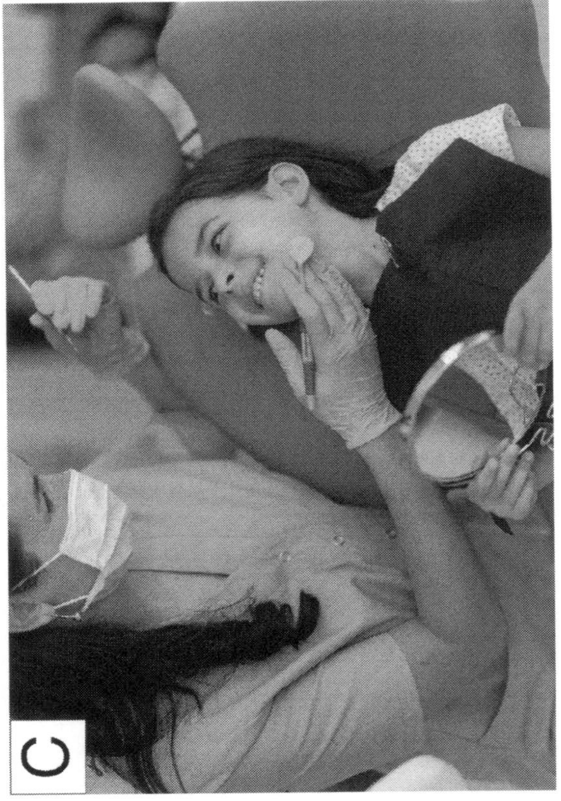
C

© Prosperity Education 2022 | 'Cambridge C2 Proficiency' and 'CPE' are brands belonging to The Chancellor, Masters and Scholars of the University of Cambridge and are not associated with Prosperity Education or its products.

Employment

Interlocutor **Now, in this part of the test you're each going to talk on your own for about two minutes.**

You need to listen while your partner is speaking because you'll be asked to comment afterwards.

So *(Candidate A)*, **I'm going to give you a card with a question written on it, and I'd like you to tell us what you think. There are also some ideas on the card for you to use if you like.**

All right? Here is your card.

Place ***Part 3*** *booklet,* ***Task 1(a)****, in front of Candidate A.*

Please let *(Candidate B)* **see your card. Remember** *(Candidate A)*, **you have about two minutes to talk before we join in.**

Allow up to 10 seconds before saying, if necessary: **Would you like to begin now?**

Candidate A

....

2 minutes

Interlocutor **Thank you.**

Interlocutor *Ask* ***one*** *of the following questions to Candidate B:*

- **Would you rather be self-employed or work for someone else? ..... (Why?)**
- **Does hard work guarantee professional success? ...... (Why? / Why not?)**
- **What's the most important quality required to make it as an entrepreneur? ..... (Why?)**

Invite Candidate A to join in by selecting one of the following prompts:

- **What do you think?**
- **Do you agree?**
- **How about you?**

Candidates

....

1 minute

Interlocutor **Thank you. (Can I have the booklet, please?)** *Retrieve* ***Part 3*** *booklet.*

© Prosperity Education 2022 | 'Cambridge C2 Proficiency' and 'CPE' are brands belonging to The Chancellor, Masters and Scholars of the University of Cambridge and are not associated with Prosperity Education or its products.

Employment – continued

Interlocutor **Now** *(Candidate B),* **it's your turn to be given a question. Here is your card.**

*Place **Part 3** booklet, **Task 1(b)**, in front of Candidate B.*

Please let *(Candidate A)* **see your card. Remember** *(Candidate B)*, **you have about two minutes to tell us what you think, and there are some ideas on the card for you to use if you like. All right?**

Allow up to 10 seconds before saying, if necessary: **Would you like to begin now?**

Candidate B

....

2 minutes

Interlocutor **Thank you.**

Interlocutor *Ask **one** of the following questions to Candidate A:*

- **What's the most difficult thing about managing a team of people?**
- **Can you be a good boss without having been a good employee first?**
- **Can employers and staff ever become good friends? ..... (Why? / Why not?)**

Invite Candidate B to join in by selecting one of the following prompts:
- **What do you think?**
- **Do you agree?**
- **How about you?**

Candidates

....

1 minute

Interlocutor **Thank you. (Can I have the booklet, please?)** *Retrieve **Part 3** booklet.*

Interlocutor **Now, to finish the test, we're going to talk about 'employment' in general.**

Address a selection of the following questions to both candidates:

- **Do managers always need to be strict with workers? ..... (Why? / Why not?)**
- **Some people suffer from stress and burnout at work. Why does that happen?**
- **Why do you think some people carry on doing a job they dislike?**
- **How do you think someone's job can affect their lifestyle?**
- **What's more important for work: having a qualification or relevant experience?**
- **Some people say that ageing makes it harder to find a job. What do you think?**

Interlocutor Thank you. That is the end of the test.

© Prosperity Education 2022 | 'Cambridge C2 Proficiency' and 'CPE' are brands belonging to The Chancellor, Masters and Scholars of the University of Cambridge and are not associated with Prosperity Education or its products.

Task 1(a)

What are the advantages and disadvantages of being self-employed?

- **free time**
- **decisions**
- **workload**

Task 1(b)

In your opinion, what makes a good boss?

- **leadership**
- **training**
- **motivation**

© Prosperity Education 2022 | 'Cambridge C2 Proficiency' and 'CPE' are brands belonging to The Chancellor, Masters and Scholars of the University of Cambridge and are not associated with Prosperity Education or its products.

Date	DD	MM	YY

Candidate ______________________________

Marks available

Grammatical Resource	0	1	1.5	2	2.5	3	3.5	4	4.5	5
Lexical Resource	0	1	1.5	2	2.5	3	3.5	4	4.5	5
Discourse Management	0	1	1.5	2	2.5	3	3.5	4	4.5	5
Pronunciation	0	1	1.5	2	2.5	3	3.5	4	4.5	5
Interactive Communication	0	1	1.5	2	2.5	3	3.5	4	4.5	5
Global Achievement	0	1	1.5	2	2.5	3	3.5	4	4.5	5

Item descriptors

Grammatical Resource *Control* *Range*	• Degree of control of grammatical forms. • Range of grammatical forms used.
Lexical Resource *Range* *Appropriacy*	• Range of vocabulary used to give and exchange views. • Appropriacy of vocabulary used.
Discourse Management *Extent* *Relevance* *Coherence* *Cohesion*	• Stretches of language produced. • Relevance of contributions and organisation of ideas. • Use of appropriate cohesive devices and discourse markers.
Pronunciation *Intonation* *Stress* *Individual sounds*	• Intelligibility • Intonation • Word stress • Individual sounds
Interactive Communication *Initiating* *Responding* *Development*	• Initiating, responding and linking contributions to other speakers' interventions. • Maintaining and developing interaction, and negotiating towards an outcome. • Widening the scope of the interaction.

© Prosperity Education 2022 | 'Cambridge C2 Proficiency' and 'CPE' are brands belonging to The Chancellor, Masters and Scholars of the University of Cambridge and are not associated with Prosperity Education or its products.

Cambridge C2 Proficiency Speaking

Test 5

© Prosperity Education 2022 | 'Cambridge C2 Proficiency' and 'CPE' are brands belonging to The Chancellor, Masters and Scholars of the University of Cambridge and are not associated with Prosperity Education or its products.

Candidates' background

Interlocutor

Good morning/afternoon/evening. My name is .... and this is my colleague ....

And your names are?

Could I have your mark sheets, please?

Thank you.

First of all, we'd like to know something about you.

- **Where are you from** *(Candidate A)***? And you** *(Candidate B)***?**
- *[Address Candidate B]* **Are you working or studying at the moment?**
- *[Address Candidate A]* **And you?**

Select a further question for each candidate:

- **Do you have a busy social life? ...... (Why? / Why not?)**
- **How much do you rely on your mobile phone on a daily basis?**
- **Why do you think art is important to so many people?**
- **Who would you like to spend your ideal holiday with?**
- **Would you ever consider moving abroad for work?**
- **What's the best thing about the area where you live?**

Candidates

....

Interlocutor **Thank you.**

© Prosperity Education 2022 | 'Cambridge C2 Proficiency' and 'CPE' are brands belonging to The Chancellor, Masters and Scholars of the University of Cambridge and are not associated with Prosperity Education or its products.

1 Class discussion – Media and information

Interlocutor **Now, in this part of the test you're going to do something together. Here are some pictures of people in different situations.**

Place ***Part 2*** *booklet in front of the candidates. Select* ***two*** *of the pictures for the candidates to look at.*

First, I'd like you to look at pictures * and * and talk together about how these people are accessing information.

You have about a minute for this, so don't worry if I interrupt you.

Candidates

....

1 minute (2 minutes for groups of three)

Interlocutor **Thank you. Now look at all the pictures.**

I'd like you to imagine that a college class is having a discussion about the media and how people access information nowadays. These pictures will be used during the discussion.

Talk together about the advantages of the media as shown in these pictures. Then decide which method of accessing information has the most disadvantages.

You have about three minutes to talk about this.

Candidates

....

Approximately 3 minutes (4 minutes for groups of three)

Interlocutor **Thank you. (Can I have the booklet, please?)** *Retrieve* ***Part 2*** *booklet.*

© Prosperity Education 2022 | 'Cambridge C2 Proficiency' and 'CPE' are brands belonging to The Chancellor, Masters and Scholars of the University of Cambridge and are not associated with Prosperity Education or its products.

1 Class discussion – Media and information

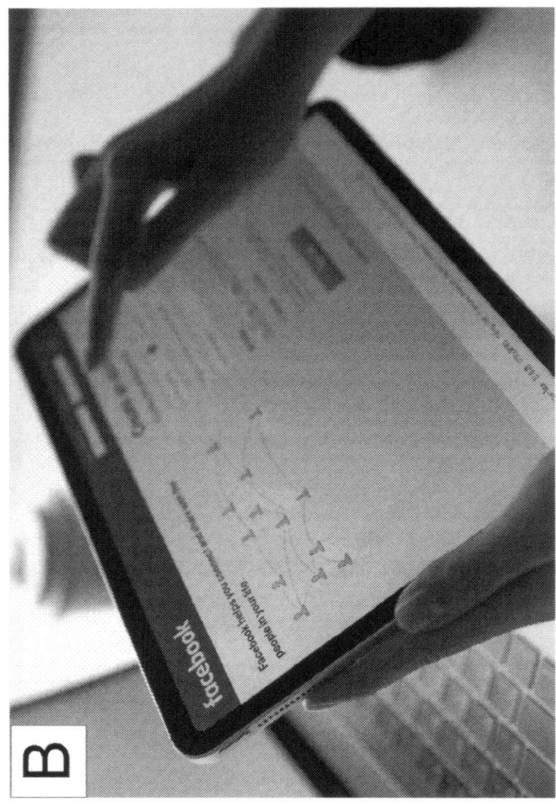

B

D

A

C

© Prosperity Education 2022 | 'Cambridge C2 Proficiency' and 'CPE' are brands belonging to The Chancellor, Masters and Scholars of the University of Cambridge and are not associated with Prosperity Education or its products.

Innovation

Interlocutor

Now, in this part of the test you're each going to talk on your own for about two minutes.

You need to listen while your partner is speaking because you'll be asked to comment afterwards.

So *(Candidate A)*, **I'm going to give you a card with a question written on it, and I'd like you to tell us what you think. There are also some ideas on the card for you to use if you like.**

All right? Here is your card.

*Place **Part 3** booklet, **Task 1(a)**, in front of Candidate A.*

Please let *(Candidate B)* **see your card. Remember** *(Candidate A)*, **you have about two minutes to talk before we join in.**

Allow up to 10 seconds before saying, if necessary: **Would you like to begin now?**

Candidate A

....

2 minutes

Interlocutor **Thank you.**

Interlocutor

*Ask **one** of the following questions to Candidate B:*

- **In your view, what are the greatest recent advances in new technologies?**
- **Should governments increase their investment in innovation? ..... (Why? / Why not?)**
- **Is innovation always a good idea in education? ..... (Why? / Why not?)**

Invite Candidate A to join in by selecting one of the following prompts:

- **What do you think?**
- **Do you agree?**
- **How about you?**

Candidates

....

1 minute

Interlocutor **Thank you. (Can I have the booklet, please?)** *Retrieve **Part 3** booklet.*

© Prosperity Education 2022 | 'Cambridge C2 Proficiency' and 'CPE' are brands belonging to The Chancellor, Masters and Scholars of the University of Cambridge and are not associated with Prosperity Education or its products.

Innovation – continued

Interlocutor **Now** *(Candidate B),* **it's your turn to be given a question. Here is your card.**

*Place **Part 3** booklet, **Task 1(b)**, in front of Candidate B.*

Please let *(Candidate A)* **see your card. Remember** *(Candidate B)*, **you have about two minutes to tell us what you think, and there are some ideas on the card for you to use if you like. All right?**

Allow up to 10 seconds before saying, if necessary: **Would you like to begin now?**

Candidate B

....

2 minutes

Interlocutor **Thank you.**

Interlocutor *Ask **one** of the following questions to Candidate A:*

- **How can innovation help with taking care of the environment?**
- **Are rich countries always the most innovative ones? ..... (Why? / Why not?)**
- **Is innovation good for underdeveloped countries? ..... (Why? / Why not?)**

Invite Candidate B to join in by selecting one of the following prompts:
- **What do you think?**
- **Do you agree?**
- **How about you?**

Candidates

....

1 minute

Interlocutor **Thank you. (Can I have the booklet, please?)** *Retrieve **Part 3** booklet.*

Interlocutor **Now, to finish the test, we're going to talk about 'innovation' in general.**

Address a selection of the following questions to both candidates:

- **Some people say that we need to innovate constantly. What do you think?**
- **How do you think the 'consumer society' and innovation are connected?**
- **Is innovation always greeted positively by society? ..... (Why? / Why not?)**
- **Will it always be possible to innovate in every area? ..... (Why? / Why not?)**
- **How can we make sure that we innovate in the right direction?**
- **Are traditions and progress incompatible concepts? ..... (Why? / Why not?)**

Interlocutor Thank you. That is the end of the test.

© Prosperity Education 2022 | 'Cambridge C2 Proficiency' and 'CPE' are brands belonging to The Chancellor, Masters and Scholars of the University of Cambridge and are not associated with Prosperity Education or its products.

Task 1(a)

In which area do you think innovation is most needed at present?

- **new technologies**
- **healthcare**
- **education**

Task 1(b)

In your opinion, does innovation always bring about positive changes?

- **the environment**
- **employment**
- **social equality**

© Prosperity Education 2022 | 'Cambridge C2 Proficiency' and 'CPE' are brands belonging to The Chancellor, Masters and Scholars of the University of Cambridge and are not associated with Prosperity Education or its products.

Date	DD	MM	YY

Candidate ______________________________

Marks available

Grammatical Resource	0	1	1.5	2	2.5	3	3.5	4	4.5	5
Lexical Resource	0	1	1.5	2	2.5	3	3.5	4	4.5	5
Discourse Management	0	1	1.5	2	2.5	3	3.5	4	4.5	5
Pronunciation	0	1	1.5	2	2.5	3	3.5	4	4.5	5
Interactive Communication	0	1	1.5	2	2.5	3	3.5	4	4.5	5
Global Achievement	0	1	1.5	2	2.5	3	3.5	4	4.5	5

Item descriptors

Grammatical Resource *Control* *Range*	• Degree of control of grammatical forms. • Range of grammatical forms used.
Lexical Resource *Range* *Appropriacy*	• Range of vocabulary used to give and exchange views. • Appropriacy of vocabulary used.
Discourse Management *Extent* *Relevance* *Coherence* *Cohesion*	• Stretches of language produced. • Relevance of contributions and organisation of ideas. • Use of appropriate cohesive devices and discourse markers.
Pronunciation *Intonation* *Stress* *Individual sounds*	• Intelligibility • Intonation • Word stress • Individual sounds
Interactive Communication *Initiating* *Responding* *Development*	• Initiating, responding and linking contributions to other speakers' interventions. • Maintaining and developing interaction, and negotiating towards an outcome. • Widening the scope of the interaction.

© Prosperity Education 2022 | 'Cambridge C2 Proficiency' and 'CPE' are brands belonging to The Chancellor, Masters and Scholars of the University of Cambridge and are not associated with Prosperity Education or its products.

Cambridge C2 Proficiency Speaking

Test 6

© Prosperity Education 2022 | 'Cambridge C2 Proficiency' and 'CPE' are brands belonging to The Chancellor, Masters and Scholars of the University of Cambridge and are not associated with Prosperity Education or its products.

Candidates' background

Interlocutor

Good morning/afternoon/evening. My name is .... and this is my colleague ....

And your names are?

Could I have your mark sheets, please?

Thank you.

First of all, we'd like to know something about you.

- **Where are you from** *(Candidate A)***? And you** *(Candidate B)***?**
- *[Address Candidate B]* **Are you working or studying at the moment?**
- *[Address Candidate A]* **And you?**

Select a further question for each candidate:

- **What type of books do you enjoy reading? ...... (Why?)**
- **How would you spend your free time if you had more of it?**
- **What are you most looking forward to in the next few months?**
- **Have you achieved anything recently that you're proud of?**
- **Where would you choose to go on holiday in** ***(candidate's country)*****? ...... (Why?)**
- **Are you fond of the internet and new technologies? ...... (Why? / Why not?)**

Candidates

....

Interlocutor **Thank you.**

© Prosperity Education 2022 | 'Cambridge C2 Proficiency' and 'CPE' are brands belonging to The Chancellor, Masters and Scholars of the University of Cambridge and are not associated with Prosperity Education or its products.

1 Magazine article – Inventions

Interlocutor **Now, in this part of the test you're going to do something together. Here are some pictures of different situations.**

*Place **Part 2** booklet in front of the candidates. Select **two** of the pictures for the candidates to look at.*

First, I'd like you to look at pictures * and * and talk together about the role of these inventions in today's society.

You have about a minute for this, so don't worry if I interrupt you.

Candidates

....

1 minute (2 minutes for groups of three)

Interlocutor **Thank you. Now look at all the pictures.**

I'd like you to imagine that a magazine is going to publish an article about important inventions throughout history. These pictures will be used to illustrate the article.

Talk together about how the inventions shown in these pictures changed the course of history. Then propose another advancement that could be included in the article.

You have about three minutes to talk about this.

Candidates

....

Approximately 3 minutes (4 minutes for groups of three)

Interlocutor **Thank you. (Can I have the booklet, please?)** *Retrieve **Part 2** booklet.*

© Prosperity Education 2022 | 'Cambridge C2 Proficiency' and 'CPE' are brands belonging to The Chancellor, Masters and Scholars of the University of Cambridge and are not associated with Prosperity Education or its products.

1 Magazine article – Inventions

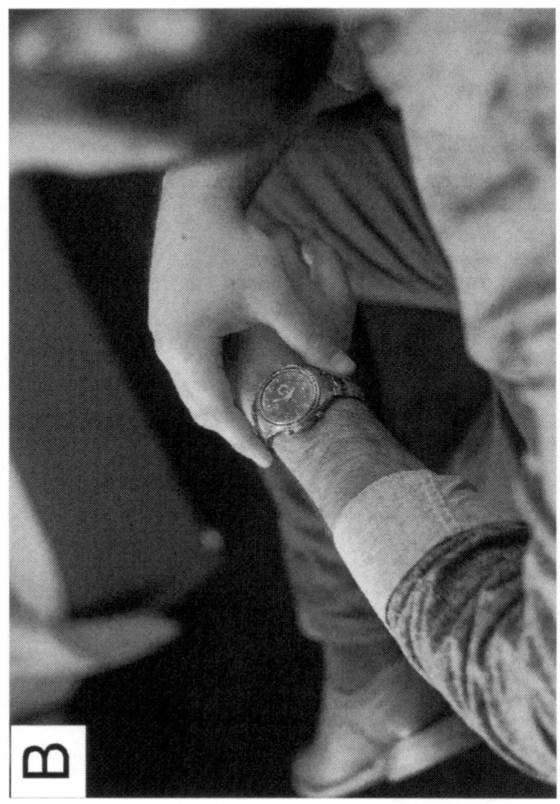
B

D

A

C

© Prosperity Education 2022 | 'Cambridge C2 Proficiency' and 'CPE' are brands belonging to The Chancellor, Masters and Scholars of the University of Cambridge and are not associated with Prosperity Education or its products.

Travelling

Interlocutor

Now, in this part of the test you're each going to talk on your own for about two minutes.

You need to listen while your partner is speaking because you'll be asked to comment afterwards.

So *(Candidate A)*, **I'm going to give you a card with a question written on it, and I'd like you to tell us what you think. There are also some ideas on the card for you to use if you like.**

All right? Here is your card.

*Place **Part 3** booklet, **Task 1(a)**, in front of Candidate A.*

Please let *(Candidate B)* **see your card. Remember** *(Candidate A)*, **you have about two minutes to talk before we join in.**

Allow up to 10 seconds before saying, if necessary: **Would you like to begin now?**

Candidate A

....

2 minutes

Interlocutor **Thank you.**

Interlocutor *Ask **one** of the following questions to Candidate B:*

- **What can cities do to encourage people not to drive so much?**
- **Should cars be banned from accessing city centres? ...... (Why? / Why not?)**
- **Is it essential to own a car in the area where you live? ...... (Why? / Why not?)**

> *Invite Candidate A to join in by selecting one of the following prompts:*
> - **What do you think?**
> - **Do you agree?**
> - **How about you?**

Candidates

....

1 minute

Interlocutor **Thank you. (Can I have the booklet, please?)** *Retrieve **Part 3** booklet.*

© Prosperity Education 2022 | 'Cambridge C2 Proficiency' and 'CPE' are brands belonging to The Chancellor, Masters and Scholars of the University of Cambridge and are not associated with Prosperity Education or its products.

Travelling – continued

Interlocutor **Now** *(Candidate B),* **it's your turn to be given a question. Here is your card.**

*Place **Part 3** booklet, **Task 1(b)**, in front of Candidate B.*

Please let *(Candidate A)* **see your card. Remember** *(Candidate B)*, **you have about two minutes to tell us what you think, and there are some ideas on the card for you to use if you like. All right?**

Allow up to 10 seconds before saying, if necessary: **Would you like to begin now?**

Candidate B

....

2 minutes

Interlocutor **Thank you.**

Interlocutor *Ask **one** of the following questions to Candidate A:*

- **Would you agree with limiting tourism in some areas? ..... (Why? / Why not?)**
- **How can tourists help preserve the places they visit?**
- **Why do some people dislike living in popular tourist destinations?**

Invite Candidate B to join in by selecting one of the following prompts:
- **What do you think?**
- **Do you agree?**
- **How about you?**

Candidates

....

1 minute

Interlocutor **Thank you. (Can I have the booklet, please?)** *Retrieve **Part 3** booklet.*

Interlocutor **Now, to finish the test, we're going to talk about 'travelling' in general.**

Address a selection of the following questions to both candidates:

- **Some people say that they can't live without travelling. Is this true for you?**
- **What do you think about people who dislike travelling?**
- **Would you rather travel abroad or explore your own country? ...... (Why?)**
- **Can you really get to know a country as a tourist? ...... (Why? / Why not?)**
- **What do you think about giving up flying to protect the environment?**
- **What kind of events can affect the travel industry negatively?**

Interlocutor Thank you. That is the end of the test.

© Prosperity Education 2022 | 'Cambridge C2 Proficiency' and 'CPE' are brands belonging to The Chancellor, Masters and Scholars of the University of Cambridge and are not associated with Prosperity Education or its products.

Task 1(a)

Why should large cities invest in different modes of transport?

- **cycling lanes**
- **underground trains**
- **buses**

Task 1(b)

What are the advantages and disadvantages of international tourism?

- **pollution**
- **cultural heritage**
- **economic growth**

© Prosperity Education 2022 | 'Cambridge C2 Proficiency' and 'CPE' are brands belonging to The Chancellor, Masters and Scholars of the University of Cambridge and are not associated with Prosperity Education or its products.

Date	DD	MM	YY

Candidate ______________________________

Marks available

Grammatical Resource	0	1	1.5	2	2.5	3	3.5	4	4.5	5
Lexical Resource	0	1	1.5	2	2.5	3	3.5	4	4.5	5
Discourse Management	0	1	1.5	2	2.5	3	3.5	4	4.5	5
Pronunciation	0	1	1.5	2	2.5	3	3.5	4	4.5	5
Interactive Communication	0	1	1.5	2	2.5	3	3.5	4	4.5	5
Global Achievement	0	1	1.5	2	2.5	3	3.5	4	4.5	5

Item descriptors

Grammatical Resource *Control* *Range*	• Degree of control of grammatical forms. • Range of grammatical forms used.
Lexical Resource *Range* *Appropriacy*	• Range of vocabulary used to give and exchange views. • Appropriacy of vocabulary used.
Discourse Management *Extent* *Relevance* *Coherence* *Cohesion*	• Stretches of language produced. • Relevance of contributions and organisation of ideas. • Use of appropriate cohesive devices and discourse markers.
Pronunciation *Intonation* *Stress* *Individual sounds*	• Intelligibility • Intonation • Word stress • Individual sounds
Interactive Communication *Initiating* *Responding* *Development*	• Initiating, responding and linking contributions to other speakers' interventions. • Maintaining and developing interaction, and negotiating towards an outcome. • Widening the scope of the interaction.

© Prosperity Education 2022 | 'Cambridge C2 Proficiency' and 'CPE' are brands belonging to The Chancellor, Masters and Scholars of the University of Cambridge and are not associated with Prosperity Education or its products.

Cambridge C2 Proficiency Speaking

Test 7

© Prosperity Education 2022 | 'Cambridge C2 Proficiency' and 'CPE' are brands belonging to The Chancellor, Masters and Scholars of the University of Cambridge and are not associated with Prosperity Education or its products.

Candidates' background

Interlocutor

Good morning/afternoon/evening. My name is …………… and this is my colleague ……………. .

And your names are?

Could I have your mark sheets, please?

Thank you.

First of all, we'd like to know something about you.

- **Where are you from** *(Candidate A)***? And you** *(Candidate B)***?**
- *[Address Candidate B]* **Are you working or studying at the moment?**
- *[Address Candidate A]* **And you?**

Select a further question for each candidate:

- **What kind of films do you enjoy watching? ...... (Why?)**
- **When is it easiest for you to relax? ...... (Why?)**
- **How do you keep up with current affairs?**
- **How often do you take a break from your work or studies?**
- **Do you consider yourself an ambitious person? ...... (Why? / Why not?)**
- **Have you made any recent changes to how you live your life?**

Candidates

………………………………………………………………………………………

Interlocutor **Thank you.**

© Prosperity Education 2022 | 'Cambridge C2 Proficiency' and 'CPE' are brands belonging to The Chancellor, Masters and Scholars of the University of Cambridge and are not associated with Prosperity Education or its products.

1 Book – Customs and rituals

Interlocutor **Now, in this part of the test, you're going to do something together. Here are some pictures of different situations.**

*Place **Part 2** booklet in front of the candidates. Select **two** of the pictures for the candidates to look at.*

First, I'd like you to look at pictures * and * and talk together about which scene you find most interesting.

You have about a minute for this, so don't worry if I interrupt you.

Candidates

....

1 minute (2 minutes for groups of three)

Interlocutor **Thank you. Now look at all the pictures.**

I'd like you to imagine that someone is writing a book about different customs and rituals around the world. These pictures will be used to illustrate some of the chapters of the book.

Talk together about the meaning of the customs or rituals shown in these pictures. Then suggest another important ritual, custom or tradition that could be included in the book.

You have about three minutes to talk about this.

Candidates

....

Approximately 3 minutes (4 minutes for groups of three)

Interlocutor **Thank you. (Can I have the booklet, please?)** *Retrieve **Part 2** booklet.*

© Prosperity Education 2022 | 'Cambridge C2 Proficiency' and 'CPE' are brands belonging to The Chancellor, Masters and Scholars of the University of Cambridge and are not associated with Prosperity Education or its products.

1 Book – Customs and rituals

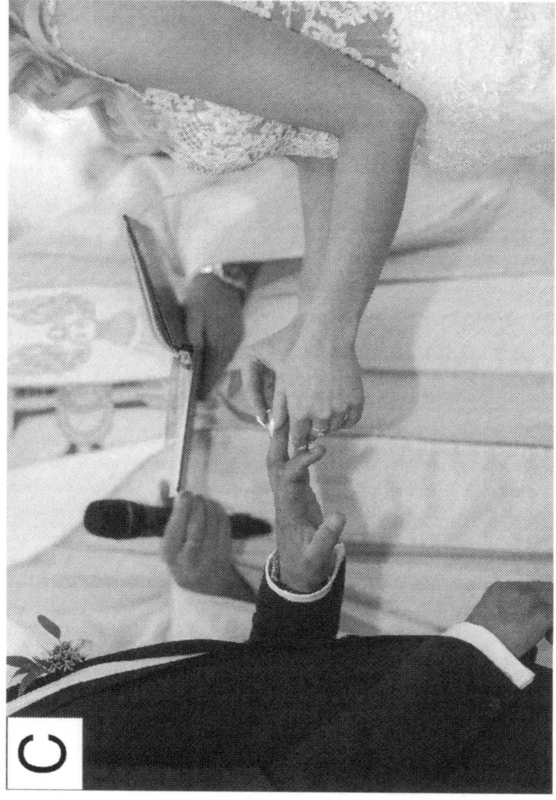

© Prosperity Education 2022 | 'Cambridge C2 Proficiency' and 'CPE' are brands belonging to The Chancellor, Masters and Scholars of the University of Cambridge and are not associated with Prosperity Education or its products.

Consumerism

Interlocutor **Now, in this part of the test you're each going to talk on your own for about two minutes.**

You need to listen while your partner is speaking because you'll be asked to comment afterwards.

So *(Candidate A)*, **I'm going to give you a card with a question written on it and I'd like you to tell us what you think. There are also some ideas on the card for you to use if you like.**

All right? Here is your card.

*Place **Part 3** booklet, **Task 1(a)**, in front of Candidate A.*

Please let *(Candidate B)* **see your card. Remember** *(Candidate A)*, **you have about two minutes to talk before we join in.**

Allow up to 10 seconds before saying, if necessary: **Would you like to begin now?**

Candidate A

....

2 minutes

Interlocutor **Thank you.**

Interlocutor *Ask **one** of the following questions to Candidate B:*

- **What comes first, consumerism or special occasions? ..... (Why? / Why not?)**
- **Why do you think most people fall into consumerist habits?**
- **What can be done to prevent consumerism on special occasions?**

Invite Candidate A to join in by selecting one of the following prompts:

- **What do you think?**
- **Do you agree?**
- **How about you?**

Candidates

....

1 minute

Interlocutor **Thank you. (Can I have the booklet, please?)** *Retrieve **Part 3** booklet.*

© Prosperity Education 2022 | 'Cambridge C2 Proficiency' and 'CPE' are brands belonging to The Chancellor, Masters and Scholars of the University of Cambridge and are not associated with Prosperity Education or its products.

Consumerism – continued

Interlocutor **Now** *(Candidate B)*, **it's your turn to be given a question. Here is your card.**

*Place **Part 3** booklet, **Task 1(b)**, in front of Candidate B.*

Please let *(Candidate A)* **see your card. Remember** *(Candidate B)*, **you have about two minutes to tell us what you think, and there are some ideas on the card for you to use if you like. All right?**

Allow up to 10 seconds before saying, if necessary: **Would you like to begin now?**

Candidate B

....

2 minutes

Interlocutor **Thank you.**

Interlocutor *Ask **one** of the following questions to Candidate A:*

- **What can local stores do about the threat of online shopping?**
- **How effective are online advertisements in making people purchase goods?**
- **Is it possible to lead an anti-consumerism lifestyle? ..... (Why? / Why not?)**

Invite Candidate B to join in by selecting one of the following prompts:

- **What do you think?**
- **Do you agree?**
- **How about you?**

Candidates

....

1 minute

Interlocutor **Thank you. (Can I have the booklet, please?)** *Retrieve **Part 3** booklet.*

Interlocutor **Now, to finish the test, we're going to talk about 'consumerism' in general.**

Address a selection of the following questions to both candidates:

- **Western societies seem to be based on consumerism. Will this ever change?**
- **How can celebrities affect consumers' decisions?**
- **Is it okay for minors to be exposed to advertising? ..... (Why? / Why not?)**
- **What can parents do to help their children develop sensible spending habits?**
- **How do you think some people end up becoming 'shopaholics'?**
- **Will online shopping ever replace in-person shopping? ..... (Why? / Why not?)**

Interlocutor Thank you. That is the end of the test.

© Prosperity Education 2022 | 'Cambridge C2 Proficiency' and 'CPE' are brands belonging to The Chancellor, Masters and Scholars of the University of Cambridge and are not associated with Prosperity Education or its products.

Task 1(a)

What role do important events or celebrations have in a consumer society?

- **Christmas**
- **birthdays**
- **weddings**

Task 1(b)

How does the internet contribute to perpetuating consumerism?

- **online shopping**
- **advertising**
- **social media**

© Prosperity Education 2022 | 'Cambridge C2 Proficiency' and 'CPE' are brands belonging to The Chancellor, Masters and Scholars of the University of Cambridge and are not associated with Prosperity Education or its products.

Date	DD	MM	YY

Candidate ______________________________

Marks available

Grammatical Resource	0	1	1.5	2	2.5	3	3.5	4	4.5	5
Lexical Resource	0	1	1.5	2	2.5	3	3.5	4	4.5	5
Discourse Management	0	1	1.5	2	2.5	3	3.5	4	4.5	5
Pronunciation	0	1	1.5	2	2.5	3	3.5	4	4.5	5
Interactive Communication	0	1	1.5	2	2.5	3	3.5	4	4.5	5
Global Achievement	0	1	1.5	2	2.5	3	3.5	4	4.5	5

Item descriptors

Grammatical Resource *Control* *Range*	• Degree of control of grammatical forms. • Range of grammatical forms used.
Lexical Resource *Range* *Appropriacy*	• Range of vocabulary used to give and exchange views. • Appropriacy of vocabulary used.
Discourse Management *Extent* *Relevance* *Coherence* *Cohesion*	• Stretches of language produced. • Relevance of contributions and organisation of ideas. • Use of appropriate cohesive devices and discourse markers.
Pronunciation *Intonation* *Stress* *Individual sounds*	• Intelligibility • Intonation • Word stress • Individual sounds
Interactive Communication *Initiating* *Responding* *Development*	• Initiating, responding and linking contributions to other speakers' interventions. • Maintaining and developing interaction, and negotiating towards an outcome. • Widening the scope of the interaction.

© Prosperity Education 2022 | 'Cambridge C2 Proficiency' and 'CPE' are brands belonging to The Chancellor, Masters and Scholars of the University of Cambridge and are not associated with Prosperity Education or its products.

Cambridge C2 Proficiency Speaking

Test 8

© Prosperity Education 2022 | 'Cambridge C2 Proficiency' and 'CPE' are brands belonging to The Chancellor, Masters and Scholars of the University of Cambridge and are not associated with Prosperity Education or its products.

Candidates' background

Interlocutor

Good morning/afternoon/evening. My name is .... and this is my colleague ....

And your names are?

Could I have your mark sheets, please?

Thank you.

First of all, we'd like to know something about you.

- **Where are you from** *(Candidate A)***? And you** *(Candidate B)***?**
- *[Address Candidate B]* **Are you working or studying at the moment?**
- *[Address Candidate A]* **And you?**

Select a further question for each candidate:

- **How long does it take you to get to work or college every day? ...... (Why?)**
- **How have your ambitions changed over the last few years?**
- **What is one thing you would never change about yourself?**
- **Do you think first impressions are important? ...... (Why? / Why not?)**
- **Would you rather own a company or work for someone else? ...... (Why?)**
- **Who's been the most influential person in your life? ...... (Why?)**

Candidates

....

Interlocutor

Thank you.

© Prosperity Education 2022 | 'Cambridge C2 Proficiency' and 'CPE' are brands belonging to The Chancellor, Masters and Scholars of the University of Cambridge and are not associated with Prosperity Education or its products.

1 Newspaper article – The food industry

Interlocutor

Now, in this part of the test you're going to do something together. Here are some pictures of different situations.

*Place **Part 2** booklet in front of the candidates. Select **two** of the pictures for the candidates to look at.*

First, I'd like you to look at pictures * and * and talk together about which picture interests you more and why.

You have about a minute for this, so don't worry if I interrupt you.

Candidates

....

1 minute (2 minutes for groups of three)

Interlocutor

Thank you. Now look at all the pictures.

I'd like you to imagine that a newspaper wants to publish an article about the food industry. These pictures represent some of the topics being considered.

Talk together about the aspects of the food industry represented in these pictures. Then decide which should be the main topic of the article.

You have about three minutes to talk about this.

Candidates

....

Approximately 3 minutes (4 minutes for groups of three)

Interlocutor

Thank you. (Can I have the booklet, please?) *Retrieve **Part 2** booklet.*

© Prosperity Education 2022 | 'Cambridge C2 Proficiency' and 'CPE' are brands belonging to The Chancellor, Masters and Scholars of the University of Cambridge and are not associated with Prosperity Education or its products.

1 Newspaper article – The food industry

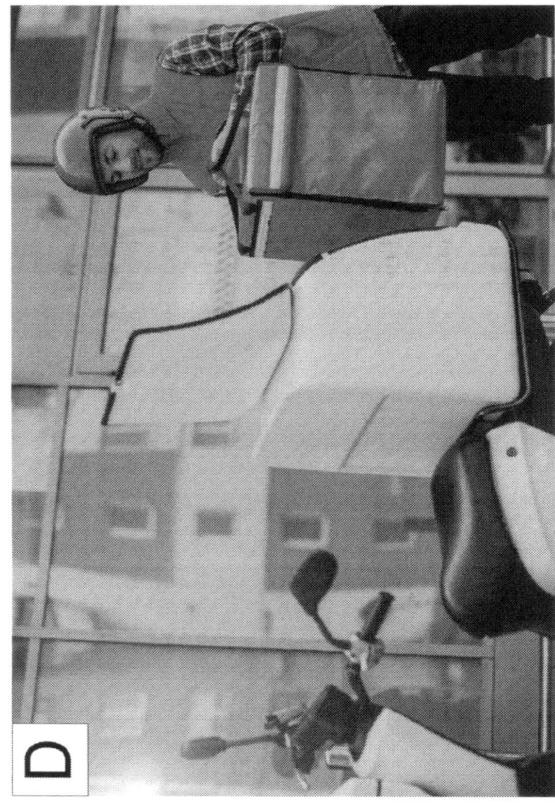

© Prosperity Education 2022 | 'Cambridge C2 Proficiency' and 'CPE' are brands belonging to The Chancellor, Masters and Scholars of the University of Cambridge and are not associated with Prosperity Education or its products.

Conflict

Interlocutor **Now, in this part of the test you're each going to talk on your own for about two minutes.**

You need to listen while your partner is speaking because you'll be asked to comment afterwards.

So *(Candidate A)*, **I'm going to give you a card with a question written on it, and I'd like you to tell us what you think. There are also some ideas on the card for you to use if you like.**

All right? Here is your card.

*Place **Part 3** booklet, **Task 1(a)**, in front of Candidate A.*

Please let *(Candidate B)* **see your card. Remember** *(Candidate A)*, **you have about two minutes to talk before we join in.**

Allow up to 10 seconds before saying, if necessary: **Would you like to begin now?**

Candidate A

....

2 minutes

Interlocutor **Thank you.**

Interlocutor *Ask **one** of the following questions to Candidate B:*

- **What should someone do if they feel jealous of their best friend?**
- **Why do you think some people find it so hard to apologise?**
- **Is it ever justified to fall out permanently with a friend? ...... (Why? / Why not?)**

Invite Candidate A to join in by selecting one of the following prompts:

- **What do you think?**
- **Do you agree?**
- **How about you?**

Candidates

....

1 minute

Interlocutor **Thank you. (Can I have the booklet, please?)** *Retrieve **Part 3** booklet.*

© Prosperity Education 2022 | 'Cambridge C2 Proficiency' and 'CPE' are brands belonging to The Chancellor, Masters and Scholars of the University of Cambridge and are not associated with Prosperity Education or its products.

Conflict – continued

Interlocutor **Now** *(Candidate B)*, **it's your turn to be given a question. Here is your card.**

*Place **Part 3** booklet, **Task 1(b)**, in front of Candidate B.*

Please let *(Candidate A)* **see your card. Remember** *(Candidate B)*, **you have about two minutes to tell us what you think, and there are some ideas on the card for you to use if you like. All right?**

Allow up to 10 seconds before saying, if necessary: **Would you like to begin now?**

Candidate B

....

2 minutes

Interlocutor **Thank you.**

Interlocutor *Ask **one** of the following questions to Candidate A:*

- **Do you think wars are sometimes inevitable? ..... (Why? / Why not?)**
- **What's more important, understanding someone's language or their culture?**
- **Why do you think some countries go to war? ..... (Why? / Why not?)**

Invite Candidate B to join in by selecting one of the following prompts:

- **What do you think?**
- **Do you agree?**
- **How about you?**

Candidates

....

1 minute

Interlocutor **Thank you. (Can I have the booklet, please?)** *Retrieve **Part 3** booklet.*

Interlocutor **Now, to finish the test, we're going to talk about 'conflict' in general.**

Address a selection of the following questions to both candidates:

- **Why do some countries intervene when there's an international conflict?**
- **Some people believe that, in war, the end justifies the means. What do you think?**
- **In your view, what's the most constructive way to prevent conflict?**
- **How can conflict at work affect a company and its staff?**
- **Should schools focus more on conflict resolution? ...... (Why? / Why not?)**
- **Why do you think so many people argue on social media?**

Interlocutor Thank you. That is the end of the test.

© Prosperity Education 2022 | 'Cambridge C2 Proficiency' and 'CPE' are brands belonging to The Chancellor, Masters and Scholars of the University of Cambridge and are not associated with Prosperity Education or its products.

Task 1(a)

What are the most common reasons why family or friends fall out with one another?

- **jealousy**
- **money issues**
- **disagreements**

Task 1(b)

What can we do as a society to prevent serious conflicts between different countries?

- **education**
- **travel**
- **languages**

© Prosperity Education 2022 | 'Cambridge C2 Proficiency' and 'CPE' are brands belonging to The Chancellor, Masters and Scholars of the University of Cambridge and are not associated with Prosperity Education or its products.

Date	DD	MM	YY

Candidate ______________________________

Marks available

Grammatical Resource	0	1	1.5	2	2.5	3	3.5	4	4.5	5
Lexical Resource	0	1	1.5	2	2.5	3	3.5	4	4.5	5
Discourse Management	0	1	1.5	2	2.5	3	3.5	4	4.5	5
Pronunciation	0	1	1.5	2	2.5	3	3.5	4	4.5	5
Interactive Communication	0	1	1.5	2	2.5	3	3.5	4	4.5	5
Global Achievement	0	1	1.5	2	2.5	3	3.5	4	4.5	5

Item descriptors

Grammatical Resource *Control* *Range*	• Degree of control of grammatical forms. • Range of grammatical forms used.
Lexical Resource *Range* *Appropriacy*	• Range of vocabulary used to give and exchange views. • Appropriacy of vocabulary used.
Discourse Management *Extent* *Relevance* *Coherence* *Cohesion*	• Stretches of language produced. • Relevance of contributions and organisation of ideas. • Use of appropriate cohesive devices and discourse markers.
Pronunciation *Intonation* *Stress* *Individual sounds*	• Intelligibility • Intonation • Word stress • Individual sounds
Interactive Communication *Initiating* *Responding* *Development*	• Initiating, responding and linking contributions to other speakers' interventions. • Maintaining and developing interaction, and negotiating towards an outcome. • Widening the scope of the interaction.

© Prosperity Education 2022 | 'Cambridge C2 Proficiency' and 'CPE' are brands belonging to The Chancellor, Masters and Scholars of the University of Cambridge and are not associated with Prosperity Education or its products.

Cambridge C2 Proficiency Speaking

Test 9

© Prosperity Education 2022 | 'Cambridge C2 Proficiency' and 'CPE' are brands belonging to The Chancellor, Masters and Scholars of the University of Cambridge and are not associated with Prosperity Education or its products.

Candidates' background

Interlocutor

Good morning/afternoon/evening. My name is .... and this is my colleague ....

And your names are?

Could I have your mark sheets, please?

Thank you.

First of all, we'd like to know something about you.

- **Where are you from** *(Candidate A)*? **And you** *(Candidate B)*?
- *[Address Candidate B]* **Are you working or studying at the moment?**
- *[Address Candidate A]* **And you?**

Select a further question for each candidate:

- **Do you enjoy attending large parties? ...... (Why? / Why not?)**
- **Where do you see yourself in ten years' time?**
- **Can you tell us about the best vacation you've ever had?**
- **What kind of company would you like to work for in the future?**
- **Is there anything you dislike about your country's culture?**
- **Is there a celebrity who you particularly admire? ...... (Why?)**

Candidates

....

Interlocutor

Thank you.

© Prosperity Education 2022 | 'Cambridge C2 Proficiency' and 'CPE' are brands belonging to The Chancellor, Masters and Scholars of the University of Cambridge and are not associated with Prosperity Education or its products.

1 Website article – Money

Interlocutor **Now, in this part of the test you're going to do something together. Here are some pictures of people in different situations.**

*Place **Part 2** booklet in front of the candidates. Select **two** of the pictures for the candidates to look at.*

First, I'd like you to look at pictures * and * and talk together about what they mean to you.

You have about a minute for this, so don't worry if I interrupt you.

Candidates

....

1 minute (2 minutes for groups of three)

Interlocutor **Thank you. Now look at all the pictures.**

I'd like you to imagine that a personal finances website is writing an article about how people spend their money. These pictures will be used alongside the article text.

Talk together about how money is being spent in these pictures. Then suggest which picture should be used as the featured image at the top of the article.

You have about three minutes to talk about this.

Candidates

....

Approximately 3 minutes (4 minutes for groups of three)

Interlocutor **Thank you. (Can I have the booklet, please?)** *Retrieve **Part 2** booklet.*

© Prosperity Education 2022 | 'Cambridge C2 Proficiency' and 'CPE' are brands belonging to The Chancellor, Masters and Scholars of the University of Cambridge and are not associated with Prosperity Education or its products.

1 Website article – Money

© Prosperity Education 2022 | 'Cambridge C2 Proficiency' and 'CPE' are brands belonging to The Chancellor, Masters and Scholars of the University of Cambridge and are not associated with Prosperity Education or its products.

Commemorations

Interlocutor

Now, in this part of the test you're each going to talk on your own for about two minutes.

You need to listen while your partner is speaking because you'll be asked to comment afterwards.

So *(Candidate A)*, **I'm going to give you a card with a question written on it, and I'd like you to tell us what you think. There are also some ideas on the card for you to use if you like.**

All right? Here is your card.

*Place **Part 3** booklet, **Task 1(a)**, in front of Candidate A.*

Please let *(Candidate B)* **see your card. Remember** *(Candidate A)*, **you have about two minutes to talk before we join in.**

Allow up to 10 seconds before saying, if necessary: **Would you like to begin now?**

Candidate A

....

2 minutes

Interlocutor **Thank you.**

Interlocutor *Ask **one** of the following questions to Candidate B:*

- **Should citizens have a say in who should be commemorated? ..... (Why? / Why not?)**
- **Can you tell us about a famous commemorative statue where you live?**
- **What should happen if many people dislike someone being commemorated?**

Invite Candidate A to join in by selecting one of the following prompts:

- **What do you think?**
- **Do you agree?**
- **How about you?**

Candidates

....

1 minute

Interlocutor **Thank you. (Can I have the booklet, please?)** *Retrieve **Part 3** booklet.*

© Prosperity Education 2022 | 'Cambridge C2 Proficiency' and 'CPE' are brands belonging to The Chancellor, Masters and Scholars of the University of Cambridge and are not associated with Prosperity Education or its products.

Commemorations – continued

Interlocutor **Now** *(Candidate B),* **it's your turn to be given a question. Here is your card.**

Place ***Part 3*** *booklet,* ***Task 1(b)****, in front of Candidate B.*

Please let *(Candidate A)* **see your card. Remember** *(Candidate B),* **you have about two minutes to tell us what you think, and there are some ideas on the card for you to use if you like. All right?**

Allow up to 10 seconds before saying, if necessary: **Would you like to begin now?**

Candidate B

....

2 minutes

Interlocutor **Thank you.**

Interlocutor *Ask* ***one*** *of the following questions to Candidate A:*

- **Should commemorative events always be cheerful? ..... (Why? / Why not?)**
- **If you could choose, how would you like to be commemorated?...... (Why?)**
- **Is it important for you to be remembered? ..... (Why? / Why not?)**

> *Invite Candidate B to join in by selecting one of the following prompts:*
> - **What do you think?**
> - **Do you agree?**
> - **How about you?**

Candidates

....

1 minute

Interlocutor **Thank you. (Can I have the booklet, please?)** *Retrieve* ***Part 3*** *booklet.*

Interlocutor **Now, to finish the test, we're going to talk about 'commemorations' in general.**

Address a selection of the following questions to both candidates:

- **Why do some people deserve to be remembered more than others?**
- **Is it ever reasonable to celebrate someone's death? ...... (Why? / Why not?)**
- **What do you think about discontinuing celebrations out of respect to others?**
- **How can commemorative landmarks be good for towns and cities?**
- **Why are celebrations like Halloween spreading around the world?**
- **Can you tell us about a special celebration that takes place in your country?**

Interlocutor Thank you. That is the end of the test.

© Prosperity Education 2022 | 'Cambridge C2 Proficiency' and 'CPE' are brands belonging to The Chancellor, Masters and Scholars of the University of Cambridge and are not associated with Prosperity Education or its products.

Task 1(a)

How should city councils decide who to commemorate in their city?

- **good deeds, historical relevance, etc.**
- **names of streets, squares, etc.**
- **local holiday, celebration, etc.**

Task 1(b)

What are the best ways for people who weren't famous to be commemorated by their friends and family?

- **annual gathering**
- **follow in their footsteps**
- **biography, website, etc.**

© Prosperity Education 2022 | 'Cambridge C2 Proficiency' and 'CPE' are brands belonging to The Chancellor, Masters and Scholars of the University of Cambridge and are not associated with Prosperity Education or its products.

Date	DD	MM	YY

Candidate ______________________________

Marks available

Grammatical Resource	0	1	1.5	2	2.5	3	3.5	4	4.5	5
Lexical Resource	0	1	1.5	2	2.5	3	3.5	4	4.5	5
Discourse Management	0	1	1.5	2	2.5	3	3.5	4	4.5	5
Pronunciation	0	1	1.5	2	2.5	3	3.5	4	4.5	5
Interactive Communication	0	1	1.5	2	2.5	3	3.5	4	4.5	5
Global Achievement	0	1	1.5	2	2.5	3	3.5	4	4.5	5

Item descriptors

Grammatical Resource *Control* *Range*	• Degree of control of grammatical forms. • Range of grammatical forms used.
Lexical Resource *Range* *Appropriacy*	• Range of vocabulary used to give and exchange views. • Appropriacy of vocabulary used.
Discourse Management *Extent* *Relevance* *Coherence* *Cohesion*	• Stretches of language produced. • Relevance of contributions and organisation of ideas. • Use of appropriate cohesive devices and discourse markers.
Pronunciation *Intonation* *Stress* *Individual sounds*	• Intelligibility • Intonation • Word stress • Individual sounds
Interactive Communication *Initiating* *Responding* *Development*	• Initiating, responding and linking contributions to other speakers' interventions. • Maintaining and developing interaction, and negotiating towards an outcome. • Widening the scope of the interaction.

© Prosperity Education 2022 | 'Cambridge C2 Proficiency' and 'CPE' are brands belonging to The Chancellor, Masters and Scholars of the University of Cambridge and are not associated with Prosperity Education or its products.

Cambridge C2 Proficiency Speaking

Test 10

© Prosperity Education 2022 | 'Cambridge C2 Proficiency' and 'CPE' are brands belonging to The Chancellor, Masters and Scholars of the University of Cambridge and are not associated with Prosperity Education or its products.

Candidates' background

Interlocutor

Good morning/afternoon/evening. My name is .... and this is my colleague ....

And your names are?

Could I have your mark sheets, please?

Thank you.

First of all, we'd like to know something about you.

- **Where are you from** *(Candidate A)***? And you** *(Candidate B)***?**
- *[Address Candidate B]* **Are you working or studying at the moment?**
- *[Address Candidate A]* **And you?**

Select a further question for each candidate:

- **Is** ***(candidate's town/city)*** **a good place for young people to live? ...... (Why? / Why not?)**
- **Can you tell us about someone you really admire?**
- **If you want to have fun, would you rather go out or stay in? ...... (Why?)**
- **What's the most difficult thing about learning a foreign language? ...... (Why?)**
- **Do you enjoy doing any dangerous sports? ...... (Why? / Why not?)**
- **What culture besides your own do you admire most?**

Candidates

....

Interlocutor **Thank you.**

© Prosperity Education 2022 | 'Cambridge C2 Proficiency' and 'CPE' are brands belonging to The Chancellor, Masters and Scholars of the University of Cambridge and are not associated with Prosperity Education or its products.

1 Online course – Tests

Interlocutor **Now, in this part of the test you're going to do something together. Here are some pictures of people in different situations.**

*Place **Part 2** booklet in front of the candidates. Select **two** of the pictures for the candidates to look at.*

First, I'd like you to look at pictures * and * and talk together about how common these situations are in our everyday lives.

You have about a minute for this, so don't worry if I interrupt you.

Candidates

....

1 minute (2 minutes for groups of three)

Interlocutor **Thank you. Now look at all the pictures.**

I'd like you to imagine that a company is developing an online course to help people deal with situations in which they are being tested. These pictures show some of the situations that are being considered.

Talk together about why the people in these pictures are being tested. Then decide which two kinds of testing the course should focus on.

You have about three minutes to talk about this.

Candidates

....

Approximately 3 minutes (4 minutes for groups of three)

Interlocutor **Thank you. (Can I have the booklet, please?)** *Retrieve **Part** 2 booklet.*

© Prosperity Education 2022 | 'Cambridge C2 Proficiency' and 'CPE' are brands belonging to The Chancellor, Masters and Scholars of the University of Cambridge and are not associated with Prosperity Education or its products.

1 Online course – Tests

B

D

A

C

© Prosperity Education 2022 | 'Cambridge C2 Proficiency' and 'CPE' are brands belonging to The Chancellor, Masters and Scholars of the University of Cambridge and are not associated with Prosperity Education or its products.

Secrets

Interlocutor **Now, in this part of the test you're each going to talk on your own for about two minutes.**

You need to listen while your partner is speaking because you'll be asked to comment afterwards.

So *(Candidate A)*, **I'm going to give you a card with a question written on it, and I'd like you to tell us what you think. There are also some ideas on the card for you to use if you like.**

All right? Here is your card.

*Place **Part 3** booklet, open at **Task 1(a)**, in front of Candidate A.*

Please let *(Candidate B)* **see your card. Remember** *(Candidate A)*, **you have about two minutes to talk before we join in.**

Allow up to 10 seconds before saying, if necessary: **Would you like to begin now?**

Candidate A

....

2 minutes

Interlocutor **Thank you.**

Interlocutor *Ask **one** of the following questions to Candidate B:*

- **Would you ever reveal someone's secret? ..... (Why? / Why not?)**
- **Has someone ever betrayed your trust by revealing a secret of yours?**
- **When is it justified to tell somebody's secret?**

Invite Candidate A to join in by selecting one of the following prompts:

- **What do you think?**
- **Do you agree?**
- **How about you?**

Candidates

....

1 minute

Interlocutor **Thank you. (Can I have the booklet, please?)** *Retrieve **Part 3** booklet.*

© Prosperity Education 2022 | 'Cambridge C2 Proficiency' and 'CPE' are brands belonging to The Chancellor, Masters and Scholars of the University of Cambridge and are not associated with Prosperity Education or its products.

Secrets – continued

Interlocutor **Now** *(Candidate B),* **it's your turn to be given a question. Here is your card.**

Place ***Part 3*** *booklet, open at* ***Task 1(b)****, in front of Candidate B.*

Please let *(Candidate A)* **see your card. Remember** *(Candidate B),* **you have about two minutes to tell us what you think, and there are some ideas on the card for you to use if you like. All right?**

Allow up to 10 seconds before saying, if necessary: **Would you like to begin now?**

Candidate B

....

2 minutes

Interlocutor **Thank you.**

Interlocutor *Ask* ***one*** *of the following questions to Candidate A:*

- **Would you prefer your government to make everything public?**
- **What kind of information do governments keep secret from citizens?**
- **What would happen if all national secrets were disclosed?**

> *Invite Candidate B to join in by selecting one of the following prompts:*
> - **What do you think?**
> - **Do you agree?**
> - **How about you?**

Candidates

....

1 minute

Interlocutor **Thank you. (Can I have the booklet, please?)** *Retrieve* ***Part 3*** *booklet.*

Interlocutor **Now, to finish the test, we're going to talk about 'secrets' in general.**

Address a selection of the following questions to both candidates:

- **How far should we go to keep our family and friends' secrets?**
- **Would it be possible to live without secrets? ..... (Why? / Why not?)**
- **Food manufacturers can keep their formulae secret. Are you okay with that?**
- **Can job interviews ask about candidates' personal lives? ..... (Why? / Why not?)**
- **What can we do to protect our privacy online? ..... (Why? / Why not?)**
- **Is it possible to live an anonymous life nowadays? ..... (Why? / Why not?)**

Interlocutor Thank you. That is the end of the test.

© Prosperity Education 2022 | 'Cambridge C2 Proficiency' and 'CPE' are brands belonging to The Chancellor, Masters and Scholars of the University of Cambridge and are not associated with Prosperity Education or its products.

Task 1(a)

How can someone decide who they can trust with their secrets?

- **friends and family**
- **personal interest**
- **professional secret (medical, legal, etc.)**

Task 1(b)

What are the advantages and disadvantages of the government keeping information secret from the public?

- **widespread concern**
- **corruption**
- **national crisis**

© Prosperity Education 2022 | 'Cambridge C2 Proficiency' and 'CPE' are brands belonging to The Chancellor, Masters and Scholars of the University of Cambridge and are not associated with Prosperity Education or its products.

Date	DD	MM	YY

Candidate ______________________

Marks available

Grammatical Resource	0	1	1.5	2	2.5	3	3.5	4	4.5	5
Lexical Resource	0	1	1.5	2	2.5	3	3.5	4	4.5	5
Discourse Management	0	1	1.5	2	2.5	3	3.5	4	4.5	5
Pronunciation	0	1	1.5	2	2.5	3	3.5	4	4.5	5
Interactive Communication	0	1	1.5	2	2.5	3	3.5	4	4.5	5
Global Achievement	0	1	1.5	2	2.5	3	3.5	4	4.5	5

Item descriptors

Grammatical Resource *Control* *Range*	• Degree of control of grammatical forms. • Range of grammatical forms used.
Lexical Resource *Range* *Appropriacy*	• Range of vocabulary used to give and exchange views. • Appropriacy of vocabulary used.
Discourse Management *Extent* *Relevance* *Coherence* *Cohesion*	• Stretches of language produced. • Relevance of contributions and organisation of ideas. • Use of appropriate cohesive devices and discourse markers.
Pronunciation *Intonation* *Stress* *Individual sounds*	• Intelligibility • Intonation • Word stress • Individual sounds
Interactive Communication *Initiating* *Responding* *Development*	• Initiating, responding and linking contributions to other speakers' interventions. • Maintaining and developing interaction, and negotiating towards an outcome. • Widening the scope of the interaction.

© Prosperity Education 2022 | 'Cambridge C2 Proficiency' and 'CPE' are brands belonging to The Chancellor, Masters and Scholars of the University of Cambridge and are not associated with Prosperity Education or its products.

Model answers

Test 1

© Prosperity Education 2022 | 'Cambridge C2 Proficiency' and 'CPE' are brands belonging to The Chancellor, Masters and Scholars of the University of Cambridge and are not associated with Prosperity Education or its products.

Model answers – Test 1

The C2 Proficiency examination is usually taken by candidates who want to obtain a C2-level certificate, which corresponds to generally native-like level of English. As described by the Common European Framework of Reference for Languages (CEFRL), candidates with a C2 level are considered to be *proficient users*, that is, users who show *mastery* or *comprehensive operational proficiency* of the English language, thus being able to:

- understand with ease virtually everything heard or read
- summarise information from different spoken and written sources, reconstructing arguments and accounts in a coherent presentation
- express themselves spontaneously, very fluently and precisely, differentiating finer shades of meaning even in more complex situations.

The purpose of the following model answers is to provide teachers and candidates with an example of language production and test performance that would score a high mark in a real C2 Proficiency Speaking test.

These answers contain grammatical and lexical features as well as a range of discourse resources suited to an advanced level of English (C2). Please note that great linguistic accuracy is expected at C2 level.

On pages 95–100, there are examiner comments highlighting different aspects of the model answers, such as:

- the strategies candidates make use of to address some of the parts
- the ways in which candidates express their opinions
- how candidates interact with one another, etc.

The aim of these comments is to draw the reader's attention to important details that might help them to achieve a successful performance in this part of the C2 Proficiency examination.

While reading the model answers and the examiner's comments, please bear in mind the following:

- The test is taken in pairs (or trios), and candidates are expected to interact with each other.

- The approximate timing of each part of the test is as follows:

    - Part 1: 2 minutes (pair) / 3 minutes (trio)
    - Part 2: 4 minutes (pair) / 6 minutes (trio)
    - Part 3: 10 minutes (pair) / 15 minutes (trio)

- These answers would achieve a high score in a C2 Proficiency Speaking test, and so should be regarded as strong-performance answers providing examples of the types of linguistic structures candidates are expected to produce at this level rather than examples of minimum performance to pass.

© Prosperity Education 2022 | 'Cambridge C2 Proficiency' and 'CPE' are brands belonging to The Chancellor, Masters and Scholars of the University of Cambridge and are not associated with Prosperity Education or its products.

Interlocutor	Where are you from, Candidate A?
Candidate A	*I'm from Seville, in the south of Spain.*
Interlocutor	And you, Candidate B?
Candidate B	*I'm from Madrid, which, as I'm sure you know, is the capital city of Spain.*
Interlocutor	Are you working or studying at the moment?
Candidate B	*Yes, I have a job as a lawyer at a popular firm on the outskirts of Madrid.*
Interlocutor	And you?
Candidate A	*Well, unfortunately, I'm currently in between jobs, but I'm actively job-hunting, so I'm pretty sure something will come up soon. Fingers crossed!*
Interlocutor	What kind of job would you like to have in the future?
Candidate A	*Well, I've specialised in website design and development, so I think a good fit for me would probably be a vacancy in an online marketing agency.*
Interlocutor	What would be your ideal holiday destination?
Candidate B	*This might sound a bit cheesy, but as long as I'm with my family, any destination will suffice. I guess anywhere in Europe would be alright, but I'd also be delighted to explore some Asian country soon; somewhere where I can experience a bit of culture shock.*
Interlocutor	Thank you.

Test 1 – Part 2

Cambridge C2 Proficiency: Speaking

Insurance company – Travel

Task 1 – Short discussion

Interlocutor	First, I'd like you to look at pictures B and C and talk together about how common these situations are when going on a trip.
Candidate A	*Would you like to kick off?*
Candidate B	*Sure. Let's see… Well, I think we can both agree that these situations are quite common when you're travelling, especially waiting around like in picture B. Whether it be at the airport or at a coach or train station, there is always some waiting involved, don't you think?*
Candidate A	*Yes, for sure. I'd say that it is kind of commonplace when flying, as delays tend to occur more frequently at airports. And… how about being a victim of pickpocketing? Do you think that's also common?*
Candidate B	*Yes, definitely. In fact, having your purse or wallet stolen is so typical as a tourist that many cities, like London, have put up signs that read "Watch out! Pickpockets about!", which I've always found quite amusing, to be honest.*
Candidate A	*Ah, yeah, I'm with you on that one. I remember seeing some signs like that in Barcelona, too. So we can assume that pickpockets taking advantage of travellers is quite common.*
Interlocutor	Thank you. Now look at all the pictures.

© Prosperity Education 2022 | 'Cambridge C2 Proficiency' and 'CPE' are brands belonging to The Chancellor, Masters and Scholars of the University of Cambridge and are not associated with Prosperity Education or its products.

Task 2 – Long discussion

Interlocutor I'd like you to imagine that a group of entrepreneurs is setting up a new travel-insurance company. These pictures show common concerns or problems that people have when travelling.

Talk together about how an insurance company can help to provide solutions to these situations. Then suggest which of these problems should be the main focus of the new insurance company.

Candidate A *Shall I go first now?*

Candidate B *Of course, go ahead.*

Candidate A *To be frank, I don't know all that much about insurance companies or how they operate, but I suppose that, as a tourist, taking out an insurance to have you covered in most of these unexpected situations will doubtless come in handy. Don't you think?*

Candidate B *Yes, of course. For instance, in picture D, where she seems to have missed her train, an insurance company might be able to help her by purchasing another ticket for her on the next train or even booking a private car, depending on the type of insurance or emergency we're talking about. What do you think?*

Candidate A *Yes, it would certainly be useful, but the problem I see here is that if it's the customer's mistake, why would the insurance company agree to foot the bill? I don't think any company would cover that type of setback if it's the customer's fault. Wouldn't you agree?*

Candidate B *That's a very good point, yes. Maybe that's not a best-case scenario for an insurance company. I do believe, however, that having some property stolen may be a solid enough reason to make the most of an insurance policy.*

I mean, if you're abroad and have your credit cards stolen, your insurance company could wire you a certain amount of money for you to still be able to enjoy your holidays until you get a new credit card sent to you by your bank.

Candidate A *Yeah, that's a good idea and something that would really make tourists consider purchasing an insurance policy. How about when there's some delay at the airport, like in picture B?*

Candidate B *Well, I know for a fact that insurance companies help in these situations. For example, say you're going to be stranded at an airport for 24 hours; your insurance company, if not the airline itself, will provide you with meals and accommodation for the night and Bob's your uncle. Luckily, I've never seen myself in that kind of situation.*

Candidate A *Neither have I, but it's good to know that someone has your back in such an inconvenient and unpleasant situation. How about when suffering an injury abroad?*

Candidate B *Well, arranging a health insurance before travelling is essential, especially if you're going to a country whose healthcare system leaves a lot to be desired, like the US, apparently.*

Candidate A *Oh, yeah, I guess it's a great idea to have your medical bills paid for you if you're in need of a doctor or have some tests while you're abroad. Healthcare is always costly, isn't it? And, if you're in a country whose healthcare system isn't very tourist-friendly, you'd better make sure you're covered.*

Candidate B *Yep, obviously. Anyway, in light of our discussion, I'm kind of leaning towards an international medical insurance as the best option to focus on as an insurance company, don't you think?*

I mean, we've all had some medical emergencies and know how important it is to have someone or something to fall back on in those situations. Can we agree on that then?

Candidate A *Yeah, you're dead right. It's probably one of the most relevant pain points tourists find when travelling, and a smart insurance company can surely make a profit by targeting it.*

Interlocutor Thank you.

© Prosperity Education 2022 | 'Cambridge C2 Proficiency' and 'CPE' are brands belonging to The Chancellor, Masters and Scholars of the University of Cambridge and are not associated with Prosperity Education or its products.

Trust

Task 1 – Long turn

Card A	**Why is it important to be able to trust the people in our life?** • **colleagues** • **friends** • **family**

Candidate A *Let's see...*

Well, let me start by saying that, in my humble opinion, being able to trust the people around you is of the utmost importance, in every aspect of life, actually.

In the first place, as far as trust at work is concerned, it's imperative to be able to trust and rely on your colleagues. Work, whether we like it or not, takes up an immense part of our lives, so being able to trust our colleagues really makes for a much better work environment, which, at the same time, affects your attitude towards your workplace quite positively. Furthermore, delving a bit more into this matter, trustworthy colleagues will look out when you feel you're out of your depth. In fact, at work is where some of the best bonds are forged, which takes me to my second point: friendships.

When talking about being able to trust friends, well... what can I say? Can you really call someone a friend if you can't trust them? It's crucial to be surrounded by dependable friends because they're the people whom we tell our secrets and ask for help and advice. Besides, not only should you be able to trust them, but also they ought to be able to trust you. What I mean is that trust goes both ways. And that's also true when talking about family, which is the last point I'll be talking about.

Our family are there at the beginning and the end of everything. They're like the foundation of everyone's life and, therefore, we should be able to trust our family the most. I mean, if I were to tell someone my deepest secrets, it would undoubtedly be someone like my parents or siblings. On the other hand, this also means that a family member could potentially cause you the most pain should they decide to betray you in some way.

Interlocutor Thank you. Candidate B, do you find it easy to trust other people?

Candidate B *Erm, I'd say so, yeah, but I'm also cautious when it comes to trusting others. Unfortunately, I have come to learn the hard way that even your closest friends can unexpectedly become your enemies. Luckily, I'm relatively good at seeing through people's intentions, so I can usually tell whether I'll be better off trusting someone or not.*

Interlocutor *How about you?*

Candidate A *Well, thankfully, I've never been betrayed by anyone close to me thus far; so no, it's not difficult for me to trust others. I believe I've been quite lucky with all my friends and relationships, so trusting others has come quite easily to me so far.*

Interlocutor Thank you.

Card B	**What can happen when you lose trust in someone or something?** • **the media** • **politicians** • **science**

Candidate B *Alright, so I'll be talking about what can happen when you lose trust in someone or something. We've already touched on that when it comes to family or friends, so I'll be focusing on other areas of trust, so to speak.*

Firstly, let's start with the media, which, as we all know, is regularly accused of having an ulterior motive or being manipulative. I won't go into how much truth there might be in those accusations, but I will say that when people feel deceived by the news or other sources of information, they tend to resort to other means or sources believed to be more trustworthy, or which are simply more in accordance with what they want to

© Prosperity Education 2022 | 'Cambridge C2 Proficiency' and 'CPE' are brands belonging to The Chancellor, Masters and Scholars of the University of Cambridge and are not associated with Prosperity Education or its products.

believe. The problem is that being or feeling fooled by the media can result in a type of scepticism that can be dangerous if it becomes widespread amongst the population.

Now, let me move on to my second point: politicians. In the same way as the media, politicians are infamous for forfeiting people's trust. I mean, they're supposed to be, by definition, one of the trust pillars of democracy, yet they seem to always end up fuelling people's mistrust in politics. There's a famous movie quote that applies here that goes: "You either die a hero or live long enough to become a villain". And I think that's what happens with most politicians; they set out with good intentions but normally end up messing up along the way. And losing trust in them, as we can see nowadays, can have catastrophic consequences in our society, as people stop believing that a fair democracy is possible.

And last, but not least, we have an interesting one: losing trust in science. I personally believe that...

Interlocutor Thank you. Candidate A, should we always trust scientific research?

Candidate A *Well, scientific research, if properly conducted and reviewed, should always be trusted. This doesn't mean that it can't be improved, expanded or, even, refuted. But any important research which has been peer-reviewed and proven to be true is always to be trusted, at least until something better comes along.*

Interlocutor Do you agree?

Candidate B *Yes, I do. As I was going to say before my turn was over, if we lose trust in the scientific method, we're lost as a scientific-based society. Science, whatever branch of science we look at, is responsible for most of the progress made throughout history, so I don't think there's any reason to lose our confidence in scientific research.*

Interlocutor Thank you.

Task 2 – Question-based discussion

Interlocutor *Can you always trust what you read online?*

Candidate A *Oh, no, definitely not! The internet is like a double-edged sword. It's available for everyone and we're all free to post whatever we want, which is great; but that's also exactly why you cannot trust most of that you'll find there, if you know what I mean. At least, that's my view. What's your take on this?*

Candidate B *Honestly, I couldn't have put it better myself. When you're online, you ought to make sure that what you're reading comes from a reputable source. And even then, it's never a bad idea to contrast that information with other so-called trustworthy sources.*

Interlocutor *Candidate B, what part does the internet play in the emergence of conspiracy theories?*

Candidate B *Well, the internet is like a free platform for people to express their views and opinions about anything they feel like. So it plays a very important role, I'd say.*

Interlocutor *Do you agree, Candidate A?*

Candidate A *I do, yes. However, I would like to add that it's the people misusing the internet to spread false information who are at fault, not the tool itself.*

Interlocutor *How does misinformation contribute to the public's distrust of news sources?*

Candidate A *Well, it's everything really, isn't it? If you realise you're being fed misinformation, you start distrusting the news, and if you don't realise you're being conned, you'll walk around believing things that aren't true. So, in a way, misinformation is the root of distrust, don't you agree?*

Candidate B *You hit the nail on the head. I don't think it would be wise for me to add anything else to that.*

Interlocutor *What can we do to make sure that we choose reliable news sources?*

© Prosperity Education 2022 | 'Cambridge C2 Proficiency' and 'CPE' are brands belonging to The Chancellor, Masters and Scholars of the University of Cambridge and are not associated with Prosperity Education or its products.

Candidate B *Wow, that's a tough one, for sure. Erm... I believe the best thing we can do is to contrast every piece of information trying to read other newspapers, for example, and determine whether the news makes sense from different perspectives. But it's still extremely difficult. What's your opinion?*

Candidate A *Yes, that's an excellent point, but I'd also say that keeping an open mind is essential, too. I mean, we tend to believe what we actually want to believe. So it is sometimes easy to be deceived if what we read or hear is aligned with our own attitudes or values. But that doesn't mean that it is necessarily true.*

Interlocutor Why do you think misinformation seems to spread faster than real facts?

Candidate B *From where I stand, I think it's exactly what Candidate A just said: we tend to believe that which we agree with. It's just easier to take something at face value when you agree with it, right?*

Candidate A *No doubt, yes.*

Interlocutor To what extent do family and friends influence what information we trust?

Candidate A *The way I see it, family and friends have a tremendous impact on the way we think and the decisions we make. Therefore, as far as trusting information goes, they will also serve as reference to determine what we can trust or not. Would you agree with me, Candidate B?*

Candidate B *I agree, but only up to a certain point. I just think that we can't generalise. For example, off the top of my head, we all know people who openly disagree about certain fundamental issues with their parents or their friends, even if it doesn't affect their relationship. So these people might not be as influenced by them as we might tend to think beforehand.*

Interlocutor Thank you. That is the end of the test.

© Prosperity Education 2022 | 'Cambridge C2 Proficiency' and 'CPE' are brands belonging to The Chancellor, Masters and Scholars of the University of Cambridge and are not associated with Prosperity Education or its products.

Examiner's comments

Test 1

© Prosperity Education 2022 | 'Cambridge C2 Proficiency' and 'CPE' are brands belonging to The Chancellor, Masters and Scholars of the University of Cambridge and are not associated with Prosperity Education or its products.

Examiner's comments

Model answers – Test 1: Part 1

In Part 1, candidates are asked about themselves, their background and experiences. These questions are scripted, and the interlocutor will never improvise them. Candidates are expected to answer and justify their responses, but these should not turn into a long monologue. If the answer given to a question is particularly short, the examiner will probably ask a follow-up question such as "Why?" or "Why not?". Therefore, candidates should answer more than a simple "Yes", "No" or one-word answer, but not much more.

For example:

Question	*Candidate A, what kind of job would you like to have in the future?*
Answer	*Well, I've specialised in website design and development, so I think a good fit for me would probably be a vacancy in an online marketing agency.*

Given the nature of the conversation, these answers should sound natural and non-rehearsed. Sounding natural is part of being fluent in a language, so using some informal expressions (*pretty sure*), exclamations (*Fingers crossed!*), contractions (*I'm, don't*) or discourse markers *(Well)* is actually encouraged, as long as they are natural and not used excessively.

As this is a C2-level speaking test, candidates' answers should show C2-level grammar and vocabulary, even in Part 1, if possible. For this reason, in the model answers provided for Part 1, there are some appropriate-level phrases like:

- *as I'm sure you know*
- *in between jobs*
- *actively job-hunting*
- *Fingers crossed!*
- *a good fit for me*
- *This might sound a bit cheesy,*
- *will suffice*
- *I'd also be delighted to*
- *a bit of culture shock*
- *etc.*

Part 1 is probably not the most suitable part for candidates to prove their level, but they should still try to show what they know, and, above all, try to sound natural.

Model answers – Test 1: Part 2

In Part 2, candidates are expected to work together on two different tasks: an introductory discussion reacting to a maximum of two pictures, and a decision-making task in which various pictures are used. They are supposed to engage in a discussion which should, if possible, culminate in a common decision or suggestion to solve a problem.

As this is a C2-level test, candidates' grammar and vocabulary are expected to be excellent and there is special emphasis on assessing their interactive and communicative skills, such as speculating, comparing, providing and eliciting opinions and reactions, evaluating, negotiating, and so on.

Notice the following elements in the sample answers on pages 92–96:

The language candidates use

If we take a look at Candidate A's and Candidate B's comparisons, we notice that they:

- **use appropriate C2 grammar and lexis:**
  waiting around … Whether it be … some waiting involved … commonplace … delays tend to occur … a victim of pickpocketing … having your purse or wallet stolen … put up signs that read … taking advantage of travellers … she seems to have missed … taking out an insurance … will doubtless come in handy … agree to foot the bill … that type of setback … provided it's the customer's fault … best-case scenario … having some property stolen … a solid enough reason to … stranded … make the most of … wire you a certain amount of money … and Bob's your uncle … get a new credit card sent to you … say you're going to … if not the airline itself … someone has your back … unpleasant situation … arranging a health insurance … a country whose healthcare system leaves a lot to be desired … if you're in need of a doctor … costly … tourist-friendly … you'd better make sure … to fall back on … pain points … make a profit by targeting it … etc.

- **express views and opinions:**
  I think … I've always found quite amusing … we can assume … To be frank, … I suppose … For instance, … Yes, it would be useful for sure … I know for a fact that … I don't think any company would … I do believe, however, … Luckily, … in light of our discussion … I'm kind of leaning towards … etc.

- **agree and disagree:**
  we can both agree … Yes, for sure … Yes, definitely … Ah, yeah, I'm with you on that one … Yes, of course … Yes, it would certainly be useful … but the problem I see here is … That's a very good point, yes …Yeah, that's a good idea … Neither have I, but … Yep, obviously … Yeah, you're dead right … etc.

These expressions show that candidates are capable of initiating, responding and linking contributions to each other's turn, and that they can develop a successful interaction and negotiate towards an outcome in a very natural way.

In this case, both candidates reach an agreement by the end. However, this is by no means a test requirement and candidates' marks will not be affected by whether an agreement or conclusion is reached or not.

Finally, it is extremely important that this part does not turn into two separate, individual turns at speaking rather than a seamless interaction. Therefore, candidates should avoid lengthy answers and should try to involve their partner at the end of each turn to keep the conversation flowing.

Model answers – Test 1: Part 3

In Part 3, each candidate is presented with a card with a question and three prompts on it. They then have two minutes to develop a monologue around the topic of their cards. This is a chance for candidates to show how well they can speak on their own in a longer turn.

Candidates' grammar and vocabulary are expected to be excellent and, more specifically in this part, there is special emphasis on their discourse management – i.e. how long they can speak for (*extent*), how relevant their contributions (*relevance*) are, and how well they can organise and connect their speech (*coherence* and *cohesion*).

Please note that even though two minutes might seem like a long time, it is common for candidates to be interrupted when the time is up before they have finished. However, this does not mean that it will affect the candidate's mark negatively, as long as what he/she has said has been delivered using C2-level grammar and vocabulary in a well-organised speech.

After each long turn, there are two follow-up questions, which give the candidates the chance to react to their partner's opinions. It is extremely important that they both pay attention to the other's monologue so that they can respond to these questions more appropriately.

Finally, the interlocutor leads a guided discussion in which both candidates are asked to answer some questions and react to their partner's answers. These final questions stem from the topic developed as part of the candidates' long turns. These are usually thematically complex questions, and they will have to answer them either individually or as a short discussion with their partner. The main goal of this task is to produce longer stretches of language as part of a conversation in which candidates show their ability to discuss a topic to a more complex extent. It is, therefore, a great opportunity for candidates to provide answers that are organised and insightful, and to make sure that their grammar and lexis are as good as that expected for a C2-level exam.

Now let us go over some important aspects to consider.

The language candidates use

If we take a look at the candidates' model answers, we notice that they:

- **use appropriate C2 grammar and lexis:**
  ... of the utmost importance ... it's imperative ... whether we like it or not ... takes up an immense part of our lives ... makes for a much better work environment ... delving a bit more into this matter ... trustworthy colleagues ... look out for you ... you're out of your depth ... some of the best bonds are forged ... ... crucial ... people whom we tell our secrets ... trust goes both ways ... the foundation of everyone's life ... if I were to tell someone my deepest secrets ... undoubtedly ... could potentially cause you the most pain ... should they decide to betray you ... I have come to learn the hard way ... when it comes to trusting others ... seeing through people's intentions ... be better off ... thus far ... has come quite easily to me so far ... so to speak ... accused of having an ulterior motive ... I won't go into how much truth there might be in those accusations ... they tend to resort to ... are believed to be more trustworthy ... in accordance with ... feeling fooled by the media can result in ... scepticism ... widespread amongst the population ... by definition ... trust pillars of democracy ... infamous ... for forfeiting ... yet they seem to end up fuelling people's mistrust ... they set out with ... end up messing up ... catastrophic consequences ... if properly conducted ... refuted ... peer-reviewed ... proven to be true ... is always to be trusted ... until something better comes along ... a scientific-based society ... a double-edged sword ... a reputable source ... so-called trustworthy sources ... who are at fault ... you're being fed misinformation ... you're being conned ... misinformation is the root of distrust ... it would be wise for me to add ... is aligned with our own attitudes ... take something at face value ... a tremendous impact on ... serve as a reference ... off the top of my head ... openly disagree about certain fundamental issues ... as we might tend to think beforehand ... etc.

- **use cohesive devices and discourse markers to organise their speech:**
let me start by saying … In the first place, … as far as trust at work is concerned … Furthermore, … which takes me to my second point … When talking about … which is the last point I'll be talking about … On the other hand, … I'll be talking about … I'll be focusing on … Firstly, let's start with … Now, let me move on to my second point … yet they seem to … and last, but not least … as I was going to say before my turn was over … as far as trusting information goes … if you know what I mean … etc.

- **are capable of expressing complex opinions, eliciting reactions and reacting accordingly:**
I'd say so, yeah … Unfortunately, … Luckily, … thankfully … as we all know … I personally believe … As I was going to say before my turn was over, … Yes, I do … so I don't think there's any reason to … Oh, no, definitely not! … which is great … if you know what I mean … that's my view … What's your take on this? … Honestly, I couldn't have put it better myself … I do, yes … don't you agree? … You hit the nail on the head … What's your opinion? … that's an excellent point … From where I stand, … right? … No doubt, yes … The way I see it, … Wouldn't you agree with me, …? … I agree, but only up to a certain point … etc.

<u>**Candidates' interaction**</u>

Some examples of good answers are the following:

Interlocutor	*Can you always trust what you read online?*
Candidate A	*Oh, no, definitely not! The internet is like a double-edged sword. It's available for everyone and we're all free to post whatever we want, which is great; but that's also exactly why you cannot trust most of that you'll find there, if you know what I mean. At least, that's my view. What's your take on this?*
Candidate B	*Honestly, I couldn't have put it better myself. When you're online, you ought to make sure that what you're reading comes from a reputable source. And even then, it's never a bad idea to contrast that information with other so-called trustworthy sources.*

In the answers above, we see great examples of interaction, linguistic proficiency and insightful answers. Candidate A reacts very spontaneously to the interlocutor's question (*Oh, no, definitely not!*) and then justifies his/her answer with a very perceptive and clever response by using the metaphor of the *double-edged sword*. To finish, he/she turns to Candidate B and asks for his/her view in an unconventional way (*What's your take on this?*). Candidate B then completely agrees with Candidate A (*I couldn't have put it better myself*) and then justifies his/her answer (*When you're online, you ought to make sure…*). The following example also shows some great interaction in Part 3:

Interlocutor	*To what extent do family and friends influence what information we trust?*
Candidate A	*The way I see it, family and friends have a tremendous impact on the way we think and the decisions we make. Therefore, as far as trusting information goes, they will also serve as reference to determine what we can trust or not. Would you agree with me, Candidate B?*
Candidate B	*I agree, but only up to a certain point. I just think that we can't generalise. For example, off the top of my head, we all know people who openly disagree about certain fundamental issues with their parents or their friends, even if it doesn't affect their relationship. So these people might not be as influenced by them as we might tend to think beforehand.*

In the previous example, we also see some interesting features. Candidate B starts by responding with a personal opinion (*The way I see it,...*) and then takes the conversation further by talking about a consequence (*Therefore,...*) of what was previously said. Finally, he/she asks whether Candidate B agrees. The latter agrees but only partially (*up to a certain point*), using an example to illustrate why he/she cannot fully agree.

In the sample answers provided by candidates, we can see that they:

- use C2-level structures
- sound very natural
- are well connected and organised
- tend to end with a question for the other candidate, which keeps the discussion going.

Finally, it is worth mentioning the presence, throughout the whole test, of collocations, idiomatic expressions and phrasal verbs typical of a native-like level of English. For example:

> *come up ... a good fit ... culture shock ... waiting around ... taking advantage of ... come in handy ... foot the bill ... a best-case scenario ... taking out an insurance ... to be stranded at an airport ... and Bob's your uncle ... in light of ... leaning towards ... fall back on ... you're dead right ... pain points ... utmost importance ... bonds are forged ... fingers crossed ... be better off ... seeing through people's intentions ... ... take something at face value ... touched on that ... so to speak ... fooled ... messing up ... double-edged sword ... hit the nail on the head ... etc.*

There are also a couple of relevant references which show that the candidates' knowledge of the English language transcends linguistic barriers and enters the cultural realm:

- Reference to a sign that can be found in some English cities: *Watch out! Pickpockets about!*
- A quote from a famous film: *You either die a hero or live long enough to become a villain.*

If used correctly and in a timely manner, this type of reference can cause a good impression on the examiners, helping candidates to obtain a better score.

Download the digital component

Downloadable content:

- Test picture booklets (Part 2)

Download url:

- www.prosperityeducation.net/speakingcpe

Instructions:

- Go to url
- Password: TIAB
- Select the *Speaking CPE* book image
- Select content to download

Printed in Great Britain
by Amazon

84822507R00061